A BEDSIDE BOOK
FOR OLDER CAVERS

BY

JOHN GILLETT

First Published in Great Britain 2013 by Mirador Publishing

First edition: 2013

A copy of this work is available through the British Library.

ISBN: 978-1-909220-75-1

Mirador Publishing
Mirador
Wearne Lane
Langport
Somerset
TA10 9HB

A Bedside Book for Older Cavers

"La vida es demasiado corta para beber mal vino"
Spanish Proverb

An Imaginary Cave System

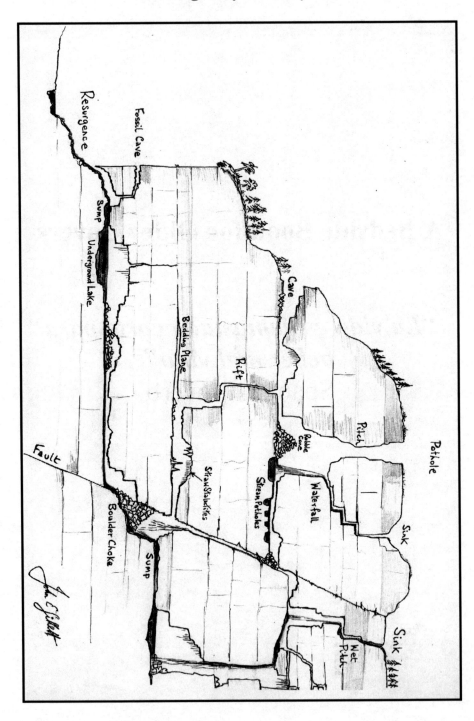

Contents

Acknowledgements

The author wishes to thank all of the friendly and hospitable people mentioned in the text, who have helped him to continue caving after the age of seventy. Their patience, support and help when the going was hard on his arthritic knees and creaking joints has been essential. In particular, Keith Sanderson, Liam Kealy, Iain Miller, 'Steve' Knox, Steve Pearson-Adams, Mick Potts, Ralph Johnson, Alan Brentnall and Javier Trujillo-Gutierrez deserve special thanks as my stalwart companions on many trips, as do the many members of the Crewe Climbing and Potholing Club who have carried my tackle bag and given me a hand on difficult climbs. I am also grateful to my wife Dilys, my daughter Catherine, my niece Alixe, Jenny and Keith Sanderson, 'Steve', Mick and Steve PA, for reviewing and helping me to edit the numerous drafts of this book.

Introduction

Seeds of the future are sown in the present. Here, you are in the present with one of these seeds in your hand. This particular seed may be stored, or sown to your advantage as you see fit. It is about choosing the best of the many paths that lead to the end of a way of life. It is a portal to the ageing caver's world and to the art of enjoying life to the full. You do not have to be an older caver to read this book, however. In fact, it will probably interest you more if you are young, or middle-aged, because it might give you some useful ideas for the future. The pleasures and pains of advancing age come to everyone eventually, so it is well to be prepared!

Our basic personalities do not change much over the years, so we need to take advantage of our mental assets as well as our physical ones, if we are to stay youthful and avoid becoming old too soon. Many older people have a young person inside them, but some really nourish this younger spirit and are not as old as their years might suggest. It is likely that older people manage to achieve this state of well-being by a mixture of physical and mental fitness, developed and maintained over the earlier years of their lives. Whatever it is, it enables those who have it to enjoy life to the full at any age.

It is important to realise that older folk possess much wisdom from their past experiences. They are time-machines for visiting the past. As people age, the memories of their youth often seem to be clearer than those of the last week! They remember that when they were young, they never thought of old age or death and just enjoyed themselves. If you are long in the tooth, caver, or non-caver, you can still be young at heart. Reading the chapters in this book could be like a sip of dandelion wine!

To those who have caved, or are still caving, this will be a bedside book, to be read by the side of a fire with a warming drink, or before turning in. The seriously hard cavers will probably have little time for it, until their joints begin to creak and they have to take life more slowly and easily. The mature and active cavers should enjoy sharing the ideas and the philosophy of living longer and having fun that are expressed in the following chapters.

This book is a collection of articles, stories and essays that were written to record caving events, or ideas that inspired the author, after reaching the age of seventy. The chapters that begin 'Once upon a time' are fictional. There is a selection of experiences that seemed to have a timeless nature and of interesting subjects that were discussed underground, or at ease after caving trips. Most of the caves mentioned are in Europe, because, after the age of seventy, the cost of travel insurance may restrict one's boundaries. Also, depending on their genes, cavers over seventy can have other restrictions on their activities underground, so the articles are selected with these in mind. In general, the caving described is in caves and potholes that are relatively easy to explore, yet challenging, beautiful, classical, or inspiring in nature. You must aim for objectives that can stretch your abilities at any age, or else you will go into a decline. Always remember that you are not so old that you have to give everything up without a struggle. This book is for those people who wish to live a life that is not as old as their years might suggest. However, it is important to remember that the ascent of six floors on foot might be a personal Everest for some geriatrics!

It is hoped that this book will inspire cavers to continue to enjoy caving for as long as possible, irrespective of their age. For non-cavers, young or old, it should provide inspiration to stay young at heart. You are unique. You have your own desires, pleasures and abilities, but here you can sample the enjoyment of life as the older cavers do! A more poetic and literate hand could describe and explain these concepts more eloquently, but, for the price of this book, let us hope that you will feel inspired, too.

1
Peak Cavern

The first caving trip after my seventy-fifth birthday was in Peak Cavern in Castleton. A dozen cavers and beginners from the Crewe Climbing and Potholing Club gathered at 'The TSG Chapel' in the village to sign documentation, pay fees and decide who was going where and with whom. 'Steve' Knox, Paul Nixon and I, all older than most of those assembled, decided to cave separately in peace and quiet. Once we had walked through the show cave, paddled along the stream-way and passed wetly through 'The Mucky Ducks', we took the lead and set off ahead of the others along the beautiful galleries that followed. We descended the 'Surprise View' ladder and made a leisurely way through the fine stream-ways, passages and boulder climbs, until we came to the 'Far Sump'.

Due to the dry spell, the sump was very low. We crouched down in the gravel to see what it would be like to wriggle through and emerge on the other side, near the Titan shaft. 'Steve' had a survey and we spent some time chatting about the passages and the route that we had taken after we had made a descent of Titan, the year before. It was quite comfortable sitting on the sand by the sump, but we eventually decided that we should make our way out to bag the best places in the pub afterwards.

We did not hurry and took time to admire all sorts of formations, pools and passage forms as we waded and scrambled on our way. Near the Lake inlet, we met the other party, on their way to the sump. We paused for 'Steve' to mend one of the beginner's lamps and then continued on our way out. The rest of the trip went smoothly and enjoyably, even the immersion up to our chests in 'The Mucky Ducks'. We were soon out into the daylight and weaving our way through the flocks of holiday-makers as we made our way back to 'The TSG Chapel'. After changing into our everyday clothes, we went to the pub for a pint together. A typical short caving trip, but a very enjoyable one!

As we sat in the sun outside the pub, with golden, frothy, pints in our hands, we reminisced about other caving trips that we had done together. However, we each felt that today's trip seemed to be one of those special, unforgettable ones for some reason. Perhaps it was the distinctive shape and beauty of the stream-ways and passages deep inside Peak Cavern? Maybe it was the sparkling cleanliness of the water, or the crunchy gravel sections, or the climbs under lofty ceilings, or even the lack of noise, that had all contributed to a special visit? Perhaps it was because we had been in no hurry and had taken that route solely for our own enjoyment? We had stopped frequently to admire the scenery and to examine particular cave formations, relishing the moments, '*To stand and stare*'. As we had caved together before, we had had a companionable journey, moving together as a single body. We agreed that the trip had not been tiring or demanding and that it was refreshing for the spirit. We felt that we were very privileged to have had the experience.

Back home, I decided to write up the trip for the club newsletter. I racked my brains to work out why such an ordinary caving trip was so different. Was it the after-glow of the Olympics? Was it because we had not been caving for a while? Was it because it was such a fine cave and such a smooth trip? Was it the nostalgia of past trips, or the effect of a pint of beer? It was something intangible, inexplicable in everyday words. It was like experiencing music or poetry. It was the mysterious effect of caving on the spirit.

Ten years ago I wrote a book about this phenomenon. I do not know if the readers found it inspiring or not. Nevertheless, the book was well-received generally. Anyway, our enjoyable trip into Peak cavern inspired me to write again, so wish me luck!

2
Caving for the Over Seventies

In ancient times, anyone who could survive for '*Three-score years and ten*' was very lucky. Nowadays, almost one in ten of the UK population can beat this target! What's more, this proportion is expected to increase as time and medical advances move on. It is no surprise, therefore, that there are so many clubs and societies for pensioners and older folk. What is a surprise, however, is that lots of them are quite interested in caving and potholing!

As a consequence, there are ample opportunities for the older caver to lecture and entertain them about this topic. The lunching, dining and charity clubs for older people have members with a wide range of ages and abilities. Most are bright and inquisitive, even though rather decrepit physically. This is due to the fact that, either they are in their nineties, or else their previous life-styles have not been healthy. The only problem is when they actually want to be taken caving or potholing themselves! It is therefore essential for any lecturer, or entertainer, to try and teach them what caving and potholing is all about in the first place. Hence this chapter:

Anyone who has reached the age of seventy needs to have a positive attitude to life in order to enjoy it. So, it is not a good idea to dwell on the physical restrictions of the over seventies too much. It is far better to concentrate on how the over seventies can best enjoy life with their remaining physical and mental assets. This particularly applies for those who want to experience potholing and caving. Potholing and caving are strenuous sports, so there will be limits imposed by arthritis, cardiovascular problems, excess weight, failing sight, poor hearing and so on. However, many cavers who are over seventy still enjoy the sport, meeting the challenges imposed by their ageing bodies as a new aspect of their caving objectives. To be truthful, unless you are fit and have lots of experience underground, caving after seventy may be almost impossible. Even if you are an experienced caver it is still quite a challenge!

At this point, the title, 'Caving for the Over Seventies' needs some clarification. In public, the media would use the title 'Potholing for the

Over Seventies', as this is more sensational and head-line grabbing. Such a title would attract more attention and interest in the street. However, 'Potholing' usually refers to the exploration of caves with deep vertical sections or 'Potholes'. Also, most of the people who explore underground systems in natural caves, vertical or horizontal, call themselves 'cavers' anyway. For anyone over seventy years old, caving is the most appropriate sport to consider. Potholing, specifically as such, involves considerable technical skill and knowledge as well as fitness. These attributes are gained by experience, so 'Caving for the Over Seventies' would best involve experienced cavers who are over seventy years old. At this point, the older folk in the audience who want to go caving will cry "Shame!" The lecturer or entertainer then needs to explain that this does not mean that people over seventy cannot learn the techniques, but it would be more difficult than the demands of less vertical caves. In any case, the over seventies can experience caving or potholing vicariously if they wish, as will be explained later. (For these reasons, this book will cover both potholing and caving using the term 'caving' for most of the time.)

For the older non-cavers, it is very important to explain to them what is involved if they really want to go caving. Here are a few suggestions:

It is important for them to understand that caving is a science-based sport. They need to learn the basics of cave conservation, limestone geology and the cave environment together with the requirements for survival underground, including cave rescue. Cave conservation is essential to preserve the wonders of the underground. In the past, many cavers were careless in their explorations and sometimes unwittingly caused considerable damage to the cave formations and environment. Nowadays, great care is taken to protect cave formations by cave conservationists from the caving clubs and speleologists. All people going underground in natural caves for the first time are specifically warned to take care where they walk and what they touch. The solution to the problem is good education.

Anyone who wishes to take up caving is advised to contact their local caving club. Most reputable clubs have a website that explains their activities and how to contact the club secretary for information. New members are always welcome and most clubs will provide tuition and caving gear for potential members. The over seventies who are still caving will already be members of one, or more, caving clubs and organisations. In fact it is often the older club members who take responsibility for cave conservation, as they have more free time. A good example of this is the conservation work done by 'The Coffin Dodgers' in the Peak District caves and mines.

It should be explained that cave exploration usually involves tracing water from where it sinks into the ground, to a resurgence where it comes out on the surface. Surface depressions, old mines and open dry caves also provide sites for exploration. Cave exploration is based on the science of 'Speleology' that is studied in many universities worldwide. The sport is driven and developed by the many established caving clubs and cave research organisations throughout the world. Most cavers belong to a caving club and participate in cave rescue organised by the regional caving clubs. In the UK, the British Caving Association (BCA) and the British Cave Research Association (BCRA) support most active cavers. The active caver population in the UK is currently unknown, but an estimate of around 7,000 seems reasonable on the basis that the British Caving Association has about 6000 cavers and about 160 clubs registered as members.

There are a few other important things to explain, too. Explain that natural caves are formed in limestone by the action of water and that there are also caves formed by lava flows after a volcanic eruption, sea caves and ice caves. The majority of caving is performed in limestone caves, however. The limestone beds in which natural caves are found were laid down over 250,000,000 years ago. These beds occur all over the World. Modern caving originally started in the limestone areas of France and then spread rapidly to Britain, Spain, Italy, America and Australia. Nowadays, cavers are active in all parts of the World where limestone is found. For example: The deepest cave in the World is now in the Western Caucasus and the largest underground chamber is in Borneo.

Natural caves, once inside the entrance, are absolutely pitch dark and cold (*7-8DegC*). Good lighting is essential for exploring caves and lights must be robust and water-proof. Warm (*usually specialised*) clothing and strong boots or wellies, plus a tackle bag for food, drink, first-aid box, spare batteries and so on, are also needed. Equipment to ascend and descend vertical drops, or pitches may also be required, depending on the cave visited.

Caves and potholes present similar challenges to those of mountain climbing. However, caves have the disadvantage of total darkness, but the advantage of walls and roofs that allow fairly easy traversing, or chimneying. Caves also have very small passages and boulder chokes, where crawling, or squeezing through small gaps, is necessary. Vertical caves that have deep shafts in them are descended on ropes using 'Single Rope Techniques' (SRT) that older non-cavers may not be able to use.

Water is often a considerable obstacle to be overcome. The caver is usually in a stream-way that may flood, have deep pools, lakes, waterfalls and low sections with minimal, or no airspace. A siphon, or sump, is where there is no airspace and the caver must dive through, aided, or unaided. Cave diving using breathing apparatus is a most hazardous sport, only undertaken by specialist cavers. Nevertheless, cave divers have discovered many new cave systems by passing sumps at the end of known caves.

Newly discovered caves are surveyed to make maps and to relate the underground passages to surface features and water flows. Accurate surveying requires a great deal of care and patience as it is often hampered by mud, water and restricted movement in tight passages. Nowadays, computer aided design systems and specialised radio-location devices have led to increased accuracy and speed of cave surveying.

For those who wish to cave vicariously, there are several websites providing useful information and virtual tours of caves. The Internet has many useful websites for learning about caving and for contacting the organisations who can help worldwide. For example:

www.swcc.org.uk
www.wildplaces.co.uk
www.trycaving.co.uk
www.caves.org
british-caving.org.uk
ffspeleo.fr

So, would-be older caver, there is nothing to stop you from experiencing caving wherever you are!

3
Blackie's Boys' Annual 1942

Once I had learned to read, I was given a second-hand copy of a *'Blackie's Boy's Annual'* for Christmas. It contained over thirty stories and articles that I read, laboriously at first, then more avidly as I became a proficient reader. The articles covered a wide range of subjects, but all of the stories were very exciting and adventurous. Just the thing for boys to read in those days, when there was no television! Even now, I can still remember many of the stories, but two particularly relate to an interest in caving:

The first story was entitled *'The Men who Froze Life'*. It was set in icy tundra, inside caverns where the temperature was extremely low, enabling scientists to freeze life and yet resuscitate individuals in the future. The caverns contained a tribe of native people who had become frozen naturally, many years before the scientists discovered the caverns. When the scientists warmed them up, they broke loose, destroyed all of the equipment and killed all of the scientists. Being frozen had given them incredible strength, but they subsequently died of 'heat-stroke' at minus twenty degrees! This story was graphically illustrated and fed my interest in science fiction in later years.

The second story was an essay by a caver of that time, entitled *'A Cave-man of Today'* and written by *'Himself'*. I have always wondered who the author was, but he lived in a bungalow next to a show cave in the Pennines that was lit by an electricity generator run from his garage. He described how he conducted parties of visitors along a plank foot-way, with all of the dangerous sections roped off. His descriptions suggest that the show cave was probably 'White Scar Cave' near Ingleton. He recounted how he and his pals explored stream-ways and passages deep inside the show cave. He also described exploring other caves and potholes locally. He explained that he recorded the findings for *'the increasing band of devotees of this new sport'*. In his opinion, life inside a mountain was very interesting and he reckoned that Ingleborough might almost be hollow, so extensive were its caves. When he went exploring underground, he wore warm clothes and his lighting was a candle stuck into his hat. He carried a meal and a flask of spirits in an oilskin bag, together with a piece of rope and the tools of his craft as a speleologist. He used to explore for up to seven hours at a time with this rudimentary gear. His descriptions of the caves were well written and unforgettable. The following paragraph, copied from his article, provides a good example of his style:

"I suppose a cave is pretty grim to most people. I love it in all its moods; for a cave has moods. It is rarely quiet, even deep down in the heart of a mountain. The only noise to break the silence is, of course, the noise of water, but how varied that can be, whether it is the chatter when it rushes over the floor of a wide cave, the roar when it runs along a constricted channel or the deep boom of a distant fall."

It seems quite extraordinary, but the words of this early caver must have existed in my subconscious and led me to take up the same sport many years after reading them. Who knows what directs the course of our lives? Although my words are not as inspiring as his were, perhaps some reader may be tempted to go caving in the same way that I was!

4
Lancaster Hole to Easegill

The underground traverse from Lancaster Hole to Easegill is a caving classic that has given many cavers considerable enjoyment over the years. Lancaster Hole was discovered in 1946 by George Cornes, when he sat down for a rest on Casterton Fell during a walk and noticed a draught coming up from beneath his feet. The initial exploration of Lancaster Hole and Easegill is well described in the book "Underground Adventure", written by Gemmell and Myers; a classic book that many older cavers will have on their bookshelves. It was in 1958 that the Lancaster Hole entrance shaft gave me my first experience of a ladder descent into a pothole. In those days, it was quite difficult to find the entrance and we had to walk down the wall as far as Cow Pot and then strike across the moor at right-angles to find it. Since then, I have visited the hole many times, as did countless other cavers and our boots eventually wore a wide track across the moor, that is easily followed to the entrance.

My first traverse was from Lancaster Hole to County Pot in Easegill, using 'Electron' ladders. The evening before, three of us walked over to Easegill and went down County Pot to fix ladders for our eventual exit the next day. We descended County Pot, then went down through 'Spout Hall', up the 'Poetic Justice' chimney, rigged a ladder into 'Pierce's Passage' and then returned to the surface. The next morning, we joined up with the other members of our club to rig the one hundred and ten feet deep Lancaster Hole entrance shaft, using 'Electron' ladder and a nylon safety rope. At that time, there was a fixed iron ladder to descend 'Fall Pot', deeper inside the cave system, so we did not need any other equipment after that. After 'Fall Pot', we took the dry route high above the 'Master Cave' stream-way, past 'Stake Pot', the holes of 'Scylla and Charybdis' and then through the 'Minarets', into the 'Monster' caverns leading to 'Stop Pot'. Here, there was another fixed iron ladder for our descent. At the bottom, we then made our way through the crawls and past 'Eureka Junction' to climb the 'Pierce's Passage' pitch and descend the 'Poetic Justice' chimney into the Easegill end of the system. We then climbed up the spout in 'Spout Hall' and continued to the County Pot pitch, where we climbed out on the ladders we had placed earlier. The traverse in those days was quite an expedition and usually took all day to complete if both ends were rigged on the same day. The larger caving clubs usually organised an exchange trip, with one group rigging Lancaster Hole and traversing through to Easegill and another group rigging County Pot and traversing in the other direction to Lancaster Hole. Since those days, the traverse has become much simpler. An easier exit was discovered at the end of 'Wretched Rabbit Passage', in the Easegill part of the system. This now avoids 'Poetic Justice', 'Spout Hall' and the constricted County Pot pitch. Also, since Single Rope Technique (SRT) was developed, the descent of Lancaster Hole is easier and quicker, avoiding the use of ladders.

Nowadays, the traverse is well within the capacity of cavers over seventy years old. This was proved on the occasion of the South West Essex Technical College (SWETC) fiftieth anniversary meet, when two of us over seventy, in the company of two in their sixties and a young caver, completed the traverse in just over three hours with considerable enjoyment!

We met at Bull Pot farm early in the morning and changed into our caving clothes. Keith and I had completed the traverse many times before. Mike and Jenny had completed the traverse using ladders in 1958. Lawrence had not been caving long, but was very fit, strong and keen to do the traverse for his first time. Keith and I were rather disconcerted to discover that the other three never used SRT and had only rudimentary harnesses, tape slings and a couple of 'Figure of Eight' descenders between them. Lots of older cavers have never taken up SRT and some determinedly resist any attempts to wean them off ladders! Nevertheless, we all set off for Lancaster Hole, with Keith and me at the front and Mike, Jenny and Lawrence following. We walked on past Bull Pot of The Witches and continued to the stile at the end of the footpath that led on to the open fell.

As we walked, Keith and I were busy chatting together, so when we reached the entrance, we were very surprised to discover that there was no sign of the others! While Keith rigged the pitch, I hurried back over the fell to find them. They had forgotten the way and walked down hill after crossing the stile! Luckily, they had realised their mistake and were returning by the time that I arrived and spotted them.

We returned to Lancaster Hole, where Keith had rigged the pitch, contrary to his normal practice, without any re-belays, to avoid having to change from one section of the rope to another past a belay. This would enable Mike, Jenny and Lawrence to descend simply on a single rope to the bottom. He had tied two plastic tackle bags to protect the rope from abrasion where it touched the rock. We fixed up their harnesses for descent so that they could share a descender that would be hauled back up the pitch for re-use after each descent. I then descended to hold the bottom of the rope as protection for Jenny, who was making her very first descent on a single rope. Looking up the shaft to daylight, I could see her coming down slowly and slightly apprenhensively. I kept a firm grip on the rope, so that I could brake her descent if she lost control. However, she came down with no problems and was very excited at how easy it was! I unclipped her descender, tied it on the rope and shouted to Keith to haul it up for Lawrence to use. He also descended with no problems, quickly followed by Mike and with Keith descending last. We re-grouped at the bottom, took off our SRT equipment, checked that our lights were working and began our traverse.

Keith led the way through to the top of the boulder slope in 'Bridge Hall'. I descended this slowly, as it seemed rather slippery and I was beginning to have the first signs of arthritis in my knees. Although I had no trouble climbing upwards, a long or steep descent made my knees quite stiff and painful! We crawled in turn through the boulders at the bottom of the chamber and went along the passage that led to the top of 'Fall Pot' in single file. The iron ladder that used to be on 'Fall Pot' had been removed, so we used a rope to protect us as we free climbed down between boulders against the right-hand wall. There had been no rain for several weeks, so Keith led us down through the boulder choke at the base of 'Fall Pot' into the 'Master Cave' underneath. We were glad to emerge from this safely as there had been several accidents when cavers had fallen down one of the drops that we had climbed past en route. As we stood on the pebble and gravel beach below, we could hear the rustling noise of the main stream. The last time that I had been here, the cave was almost in flood, with water flowing over the beach and the roar of the current, crashing against the cave walls and swirling over submerged rocks, was deafening. Today, the stream-way was a pleasure to be in after the muddy passages and boulders above. The stream ran along a beautifully scalloped passage, about five metres high and four wide, with occasional deep pools, small waterfalls and bends, where the current made the water rise up one side of the passage. We made good progress, enjoying the rush and refreshing spray of the water, wading through the deeper pools and stopping occasionally to look at the flowstone and stalactites that decorated the passage. Once we had negotiated the boulder collapse area beneath 'Stake Pot', the roof lifted and was soon high above us. The 'Master Cave' was such a pleasure to be in and so much more beautiful than the overhead dry route. Eventually we had to climb out of the water and upwards through a boulder choke across the passage to 'Oxbow Corner', the next key point on our traverse. I was glad that Keith was leading us here. Every time in the past that I had been in the lead here, I had had some difficulty deciding the best place to start the climb up through the boulders. The climbing and wriggling was very energetic, so we were all glad to pause for breath at the top, eat some chocolate and take a drink of water, sitting on the muddy banks high above the 'Master Cave'.

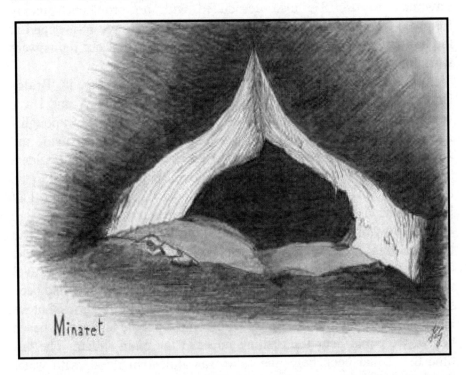

Minaret

We were now about half way through our traverse. A low crawl led to a small chamber and then enlarged considerably as we entered 'Oakes Cavern'. Across this cavern, the way came to an abrupt end. We had reached the start of 'The Minarets'. The 'Minarets' are an unforgettable sight. They have a cross-section shaped just like the pointed, onion-shaped, top of a minaret. They run parallel to each other, with low, short crawls to connect them. We walked and crawled until we were able to climb out the other side into the enormous

'Cornes Cavern'. This cavern is huge and often called 'The Monster Cavern'! Although it is possible to walk down and along the bottom of this chamber, we traversed the sloping muddy sides, that were slippery in places, to get a better view and quicker progress. At the far end, 'Cornes Cavern' narrowed and then the passage size increased again as we entered 'Snail Cavern'. We crossed this cavern and took a passage on the left, where we had to climb over and around several large boulders to reach the top of 'Stop Pot'.

'Stop Pot' still had its fixed iron ladder in place, although it involved a few delicate manoeuvres to reach the top rung safely. The ladder rested at the top of a large boulder slope that was above another stream-way called 'The Main Drain'. We scrambled down to the stream and Keith led the way into a low crawl that eventually emerged at 'Eureka Junction'. We followed this upstream and took a left turn into 'Wretched Rabbit' passage. This passage was avoided in the past because of its narrowness, exacerbated by continual twisting and turning from side to side. However, we followed this as it gradually rose towards a high rift chamber. Here, we climbed up the rift, with our overalls catching on projections and with much puffing and grunting from our exertions. Finally, there was a pitch upwards in three separate steps. Keith climbed up first, taking a rope in his tackle bag for anyone who needed help on the climbs. Needless to say, I was now quite tired and the most decrepit of our team. I managed the first step, but could not get my left knee to bend enough for me to reach a foothold on the second one. Luckily, I received a bunk up from Lawrence to overcome this problem. The top climb was fairly easy and, shortly afterwards, we emerged into daylight on the bank of Easegill.

We sat in the sun for a while and chatted about our experiences enthusiastically before setting off over the fell to de-rig Lancaster Hole. The walk seemed longer, but more enjoyable than usual to me. Keith and Lawrence walked ahead at full speed, leaving Mike, Jenny and me to take our time. We had lots to discuss, particularly the SWETC Anniversary events to come. Almost a hundred members were camped at the Dalesbridge campsite near Clapham to celebrate, starting with a barbecue in the evening. By the time that we reached Lancaster Hole, Keith and Lawrence had de-rigged the pitch and were ready to leave, so we walked back to Bull Pot Farm with them to clean our gear and get changed. By common consent, we then drove down to the nearest pub for a celebratory drink together.

Keith and I had never caved with Mike, Jenny and Lawrence before, so, as we drank our beers and chatted in the bar, we were surprised to discover that we had all studied science. In my experience, most of the cavers that I have met have been technologists or engineers of some sort. Caving does not seem to attract as many classical scholars as scientists! Mike, Keith and Jenny were physics teachers, Lawrence was a mathematician and I was a chemical engineer. Lawrence and I discovered that we both spoke French and, as physics teaching began to dominate the conversation, Lawrence and I conversed in French about other topics. Time passed very quickly and our enjoyment was only terminated by the fact that two of us had to drive back to Clapham without being over the alcohol limit. We had to be back in time for the SWETC Anniversary barbecue that evening!

Another most enjoyable caving trip for us to remember. We were all pleased to have completed it without any problems and much enjoyment. It certainly gave those of us who might be considered to be older cavers a good reason to continue caving for as long as we possibly could!

5
Experience

"Ride the roller coaster for a fantastic experience!" "Taste the terror of the Space Mountain!" "Experience the hair-raising Zip Wire!" "Scream in the Ghost Train!" The advertisements for fairground rides and amusement parks all promise an experience, albeit ephemeral! People are prepared to queue and pay for such thrills, so they must think it worthwhile. However, there are other experiences of a more rewarding and educational nature to be had. Caving is one of them.

Caving is an experience that affects people in many different ways and from many different aspects. For the beginner, this experience is often tinged with the fear of the unknown or of any obvious hazards that may be encountered. For the regular caver there is always the pleasure of visiting another world, tinged with the excitement of overcoming particular challenges, especially if there is the opportunity for new discoveries. For the older caver there will be the pleasure of revisiting old routes as well as the anticipation and excitement of finding new routes, tinged with the challenges presented by a reduction in physical ability. For non-cavers, caving is a concept only, with any knowledge often governed by the exaggerated opinions of the media. Non-cavers frequently say that caving is something to be avoided and they often express a fear of tight places and of getting stuck underground. For anyone with no real caving experience, caving is an unknown entity.

Our awareness of the world around us is governed largely by our minds. For example, it takes a significant time for the light from an object that we are looking at to register on the retina. It takes further time to transfer the retinal image to the brain where it takes time to process this and allow our perception to be completed. In all, it can take almost half a second to see something, so we always live in the past! Another example of the way that time affects our perception is when we look up at the night sky. Light travels at a finite speed and this has a considerable effect over great distances. The light from the stars that we see in the sky was transmitted many years ago, so we see the stars in the sky as they were in the past. They are no longer there and we are looking at their history! These two examples indicate that, because our sensory systems take a finite time to work, our awareness and understanding of the world around us is limited. We have to depend on the images and models stored in our brains.

We can perceive the world around us by other means than by light. We hear using sound-waves in our ears. We feel things with our fingers. We taste things with our tongue and smell things with our nose. In each case the information has to be processed by the brain, producing a finite time lag. Although we are restricted by our five senses, we can use specialised instruments to augment them. The development of telescopes and microscopes extended our spatial field of view considerably. Spectroscopes extended our view across the electro-magnetic spectrum outside the range of our eyes. Likewise instruments to study electro-magnetic fields and radiation, gravitational fields and forces, nuclear fields, atomic and molecular structures have extended our perception of the world around us enormously. The ancients did not have these wonderful devices and had to rely on their primitive senses and experience to guess at how the world worked. This led to all sorts of ideas and hypotheses about the world that could not be tested. For example, it was assumed that the world was flat for centuries! There was, however, a perception of the occult derived from the effects of heightened states of consciousness or of naturally occurring drugs. This led to the development of rituals and religions based on their beliefs at that time.

We all regard things differently, depending on our education and experience. Reality is a difficult subject to describe and, as T.S.Eliot said, "Humankind cannot bear very much reality". Existentialists consider that reality cannot be understood except by direct experience. Philosophising about reality will get you nowhere! This is particularly true in the case of caving. The physical and mental effort required to complete a caving trip endows the caver with a direct awareness of reality. Concentrating on a difficult manoeuvre, high above a deep pitch, totally focuses the mind and body on the task in hand. Squeezing through a tight constriction requires the same level of attention, to the exclusion of everything else. Passing through a watery crawl with a very small airspace, requires careful movement and a calm state of mind to avoid ingesting water or even drowning.

When someone is described as 'experienced', it is usually assumed that the person has practised whatever task or sport that he, or she, is undertaking many times and can be expected to perform it competently, safely and effectively. Experienced people have always undergone training, education and 'rites of passage'. They have learned how to overcome hardships and obstacles in the way of their objectives. Experienced people have a sense of perfection, know all of the short cuts, know all the 'tricks of the trade' and can assess and control any risks involved. There is something to beware of, however. "Time-serving" is not the only criterion for getting experience. It is quite possible for people to have performed some activity for a long time, but without gaining any benefit or useful experience. Nevertheless, any caver who has spent more than twenty years caving is usually experienced as it unlikely that he or she learned nothing in all that time. The time served has to be well spent and educational to generate experience. There has to be recognition and a mindful awareness of the experience for the person to benefit. In the final analysis, anyone who claims to be an 'experienced' caver can quickly be recognised by his, or her, actions underground. As in the professions, where candidates for admission have to pass examinations and have their practical experience monitored, cavers can undergo formal training and education in the sport at recognised cave training centres. Additionally, there is a well accepted certification system for cave trainers and leaders. However, the majority of older cavers never had these opportunities and were completely self-taught, or learned the sport with a mentor, so you have to take their experience on trust.

The caving experience is recognised by many organisations as a means of developing leadership skills and as a means of helping people develop self- confidence. There are many organisations that use caving effectively and wisely to develop their members of staff. Unfortunately some may perform this service badly, to the extent that young apprentices endure experiences that may endanger their lives, or put them off caving forever. Additionally, cave conservation may not be emphasised sufficiently and cave formations may be damaged due to ignorance. In the opinion of the author, caving should be undertaken with a real personal interest in the sport and with care to preserve the underground environment. The caving experience is a very special experience with many complex personal benefits that are not gained by coercion.

It is interesting to note that blind people who have experienced caving not only gain a wonderful and different insight to the underground world, but that they communicate their different perceptions to their guides. Several cavers who have guided blind people underground have remarked that they had not really been aware of all sorts of senses when they caved themselves. The blind cavers taught them to listen to the texture of the ground underfoot, from splashing in puddles, streams or pools of water, to crunching over the gravel in streambeds and the echoes of footsteps in passages of different size or shape. They also learned to listen to the drips from the roof, to smell the mud, the rock and the water vapour in the air. Losing one of the senses makes those remaining more sensitive.

The experienced older caver will have a good working knowledge of limestone geology and cave formation, cave conservation, cave exploration, caving equipment, first-aid, cave rescue and will have caved in many caves in different regions worldwide. Additionally, older cavers often settle in a particular region and become expert in the local caves and in their conservation. Others may have specialised knowledge of the various scientific caving activities such as cave biology, hydrology, cave surveying, photography and archaeology. Although academic knowledge is transferable, experience is a personal non-transferable asset that can only be gained by living with an awareness of the world in which it is gained. Experience is a multi-faceted asset and older cavers usually possess plenty of it! In the final years of an older caver's career, experience really counts as it allows a continuing enjoyment of the wonderland under the ground.

6
Caving in Burgundy

Burgundy is one of the most beautiful and interesting regions in France, with many historic buildings, forests, wooded hills, vineyards, delicious food and friendly people. In addition, the Burgundy Côte D'Or is limestone country. Limestone cliffs abound and there are over thirty significant cave systems on record, ranging from 16km. in length to 72m. in depth. For the older caver, Burgundy is a veritable paradise for living and caving.

Every year, Dilys and I go there to stay with our caving friends, Yannick and Claude Bonvalot. Apart from eating, drinking and loading up our boot with Burgundy wine and food, we usually go walking or caving together. Every other year they visit us in the Peak District, for a similar purpose.

One year, in July, Yannick and I went into La Grande Dore, a cave below the cliffs near Bouilland, not far from where he lives. The year before, when we had visited the cave, it had been raining for a fortnight. Water was springing out of holes in the ground as we walked uphill to the cave entrance. The cave entrance was dry, but, as we crawled over boulders to reach the main passage, we could hear the stream with its roaring voice echoing through the cave. As we advanced, it was clear that the cave was in flood! Nevertheless, we ventured further in and managed to traverse above the water, in a dry rift with jagged projections that tore a pocket off my old boiler suit! We struggled quite a way upstream until the passage became impassable due to the water level and we had to abandon the trip. A year later, however, the weather was dry and we succeeded in reaching the final siphon, about a quarter of a mile in.

La Grande Dore has been formed along a major joint in thickly bedded limestone. The cave entrance is in a wood, at the base of a limestone cliff that borders a large field. A steep scramble over boulders and under overhanging trees leads to a low entrance. Access to the stream-way is over boulders, where we had to stoop and crawl forward through a low chamber. We followed the stream a short way, via several constrictions and then climbed up into a rift passage, traversing on ledges occasionally, with short climbs and descents over and down to the stream. After about 250m, Yannick climbed down a tricky descent over a deep pool to a junction that had been under water last year. He then tried to continue along the rift at water level, but missed the way on. I climbed down behind him and, as the rift was too narrow for him to return and pass me, found the low duck that he had missed. It only had a few inches of airspace and I could not be sure that it led to a larger passage beyond. Anyway, the water was crystal clear and not too cold, so I ducked under, getting an ear-full in doing so, to surface in a large passage. Yannick quickly joined me and we explored a delightfully clean stream-way to the final siphon. Yannick was very pleased. It was the first time that he had been able to reach this siphon for many years! We made our return with no problems and took a different route out, through a low, watery, passage over which we had traversed on the way in. We emerged, wet, but clean and ready for a glass of '*Vin Nois*' for an aperitif, followed by a bottle of Hautes Côtes de Beaune red with the picnic lunch that Claude and Dilys had prepared for us on the surface.

The next day, we all went to visit the Grottes d'Azé, near Cluny. These show caves had been explored by Burgundian cavers in the sixties and many important prehistoric finds were recovered by archaeologists. Cavers and archaeologists are still excavating new passages in the caves, which now have several miles of accessible passages. There is a very good museum that displays many of the artefacts and bones that were recovered from the caves, as well as videos, maps and photographs of the system.

There are two caves at Azé, an active river cave with both tourist and 'wild' sections, and a prehistoric cave situated above this. Yannick, Claude and their two daughters were great friends of the cave owners and had all been involved in exploration and as guides over the years. Patrick, Yannick's brother-in-law, was on guide duty when we arrived as it was a busy weekend for tourists. Yannick obtained a key and led us on a private visit, counter-current to the tourists, through the river cave and then through the upper prehistoric cave. Our trip was most enjoyable and interesting and lasted almost two hours. The cave is well worth a visit for older cavers who are visiting the area.

In 1973, Yannick, Patrick and local cavers started to explore La Molle Pierre, a cave in a limestone cliff, located in the wooded hills between the villages of Bouze-les-Beaune and Mavilly-Mandelot. The cave entrance had been used for many years as a refuge for animals and hunters and was reputed to have been much larger in the past. They removed clay and rocky infill at the back of the cave and managed to pass several squeezes and boulders to gain access to the rest of the cave system. They soon began to unearth pieces of pottery, bone and other archaeological objects. They quickly realised the importance of their find and digging was suspended while professional archaeologists were contacted. In 1983, a carefully planned archaeological dig was organised, starting in a small chamber twelve metres inside the entrance. Platforms, ladders, electric lighting and rails to remove the debris were installed to aid the diggers and research workers. The whole site was marked out and photographed, to identify accurately where items were found. The professional archaeologists removed many artefacts from the dig over a period of about seven years. Neolithic, Roman-Gallic and Medieval artefacts were removed, along with bones and wastes from animals that had used the cave as a lair. Most of these are now exhibited in a museum in nearby Beaune.

Once the archaeological work had finished, the cavers continued their digging explorations, opening up deep rifts and clearing sediments, boulder chokes and squeezes, to extend the cave considerably. Dilys and I visited the cave with them on several of their working Sundays over the years. We always enjoyed the 'dejeuner sur l'herbe' afterwards! A serious digging session and extended lunch was arranged to celebrate my seventy fifth year. We made an early start and a generator was positioned at the top of the cliff to feed a cable that was run down to the entrance. We all made our way through the low trees and bushes to descend the cliff by a ladder. Below, a footpath led along a wide ledge under the trees to the cave entrance. Patrick unlocked the entrance and removed various items of steel and heavy equipment used to deter vandals from gaining access.

Once the entrance was clear, we sat on the rocks outside to discuss the work programme. Michel Doublot opened a bottle of white wine from the Savoie and we each took a glass to toast and lubricate our efforts. Then the generator was started to provide electric lighting at the dig face. Additional lights also illuminated a deep shaft to an abandoned dig that ended in an impassable squeeze that was awaiting attack by experts with explosives. Inside the cave there was an overhead rail, about sixty metres long, to transfer buckets of spoil from the current dig at the far end of the system, to be emptied into another abandoned dig near the entrance. Patrick and Michel worked at the face, Yannick and I broke up rocks and loaded the spoil into buckets. Titouan, Yannick's nephew, slung the buckets on to hooks on the overhead rail. Marise and François pulled the buckets across and emptied them before returning them to the dig face again. The digging went with a swing and continued until mid-day. The work was quite hard, but luckily for me, the team had a regular routine that always ended at noon. At noon, we returned to the top of the cliff for lunch. It was a lovely sunny day. Brightly coloured flowers dotted the grass and scented the warm air. In a clearing among the oak, hornbeam, beech trees and hazel bushes, the ladies had laid a table and were busy opening cool-boxes, warm-boxes and interesting bags and packets of food for us.

Each of the wives had provided a separate course and the men had provided wines, so we had plenty to eat and drink. We washed our hands and sat down around the table. The lunch started with an *aperitif* that was a cocktail of chilled rosé wine and a pink grapefruit liqueur. To go with this, there were *amuses-bouches*, that consisted of slices of *saussison*, radishes, *cornichons*, and plenty of fresh bread. We sipped our drinks, nibbled the canapés and chatted amiably, until it was time for the lunch proper. The starter, provided by Marise, was *Jambon persillé*, a local delicacy of ham and parsley in aspic, eaten with more bread and various pickles. A chilled white wine from the Jura accompanied this. The number of conversations multiplied and so did the noise volume as the wine took effect. We exchanged news since our last reunion, recalling people and shared experiences above and below ground. Then there was the main course to eat. Claude served sliced *Gigot* of lamb that she had roasted earlier and kept warm in an insulated container. This was accompanied by a *ratatouille*, provided by Marie-Jo, Yannick's sister and a salad by Marise. Yannick and Michel served two red wines to drink with this, an Haute Cotes de Beaune and a Pernand Vergelesse. The cheeses were tabled after the salad: *Comté, Munster, Bleu de Bresse, Chaource, Brébis, Chêvre* and, our offering; Stilton. Once the Burgundy reds had been consumed, Patrick provided a heavier red from Bordeaux to match the more powerful cheeses. Finally we had dessert: *Clafoutis* (Cherry tart) provided by Sylvie, Michel's partner, and a ginger cake, provided by Marie-Claire. In addition, Marie-Jo had baked a birthday sponge cake for her son, Titouan, the youngest caver. He celebrated his birthday by serving us all with a fine sparkling *Crémant de Bourgogne* to go with the cake. With the coffee, there was *Tanaisie,* a strong, herby, liqueur that Yannick had made. A warm silence enveloped the table as we all sat back digesting a most enjoyable meal in the open air. A most satisfying and enjoyable way for older cavers to complete a caving trip!

After lunch, the cavers returned to work for another hour or so while the ladies cleared the table. As the senior persons present, Dilys and I were excused, so we took a siesta in the shade! One has to take benefits of age whenever they become available, especially after such a delicious lunch! Eventually I went down to lend a hand, arriving just before the work ended. Once the dig face had been cleared and the buckets and so on tidied, Patrick and Michel closed up the cave entrance to protect it from vandals. We all returned to the top of the cliff to switch off the generator and pack up the equipment. Soon we were saying farewells after a splendid day together. We left for home in the late afternoon sun, soaking up the warm and mellow atmosphere. Such days should be bottled up for future pleasure!

Apart from the many limestone caves, Burgundy has many caves of a different nature, particularly interesting to the older caver. These caves (*Pronounced 'carves'*) are wine cellars! A visit to one of these is a must for anyone visiting the region. These *caves* are underground, with low lighting, chilly temperature, yeasty scents and with side chambers and passages lined with barrels and bottles. They have an atmosphere redolent of limestone caves and late-night pubs. Every year, we visit one of these *caves* in the village of Nantoux for a *'degustation de vins'*. The vintner, Christian Menaut, is a local singer who has a good voice and lots of amusing anecdotes to recount to French-speaking visitors. Most of his vines are on the 'Hautes Cotes' nearby, with particular vineyards, 'La Jolivode' and 'Beauregarde' on the hill between Nantoux and Bouze-les Beaune, growing the Pinot Noir grape. Christian also has vignobles in Beaune, Pommard and Montrachet. However, Nantoux is one of the best sources of the white grape Aligote, used to make the aperitif 'Kir' (*Named after Canon Kir of Dijon, who invented it to increase the sales of Dijon Cassis!*). Christian's Aligote can be used to make 'Kir', but is also a fine dry wine that goes well on its own with seafood and fish. Our visits to his *cave*, with Yannick and Claude, would usually take about two hours and always prove to be very enjoyable! When the wines that we wanted had not yet been bottled, Christian would use a pipette for us to sample it from the oak barrel. (Yannick would then ferry it home for us later in the year, when he and Claude visited us in England). We always return home with several crates of his wine, as Christian certainly knows how to bottle up the summer! Whenever we open a bottle of Burgundy, the essence of such days is always there to be savoured.

7
Uncertainty

"Watch out!" "Caillooooo-ou!" "Wheeee!" "Splat!" A stone whizzed down the pitch from high above us and shattered on the floor! "Holy crumpet!" My companion observed, wiping a cut on his cheek from a flying stone chip. "Lucky that missed! It could have killed someone!"

When we go caving, we expect to return safely to the surface. We have faith in our physical strengths, skills and knowledge to do so, but sometimes we make mistakes. We may get lost and tired out. We may underestimate the rise in water levels and get trapped, or drown. We may disturb loose boulders and get crushed. We may squeeze into a tight crawl and get stuck. We may not put on effective clothing, get cold and wet and suffer hypothermia. We may slip and fall from height. We may not rig our rope systems properly and have trouble getting back up, or let abrasion break them. Our personal equipment, particularly our light, may fail when least expected. Let's face it; with this degree of uncertainty, we need to be very careful when we go caving!

We live in a world shrouded in uncertainty. In spite of the best efforts of scientists and mathematicians, the tools available to quantify and reduce uncertainty are still difficult to use and of limited application. As a result, most people confronted by uncertainty have to trust the advice of the experts, or to rely on their own judgement. History, however, records countless disasters that show human judgements about probability are extremely prone to error! "Taking a chance," or gambling, is often the way to misfortune.

The problem of uncertainty is a human one. When we take risks relating to ourselves, we tend to emphasise the benefits and ignore the worst that could happen to us. When the benefits are for society and the consequences of taking the risk are unknown, or catastrophic, we emphasise the consequences and ignore the likelihood of the event, even though it might be extremely small. This trait prompted the definition of "The Precautionary Principle" that is often used by environmentalists, bureaucrats and others to prevent risky activities and experiments that could be of long term benefit to mankind. Although there is useful knowledge to quantify uncertainty, its application is limited by widespread ignorance about probability and statistics. The media frequently exploit this ignorance, to misrepresent and sensationalise events and decisions involving risk. In the hands of the media and politicians, uncertainty is the power that enables them to lead their audience by the nose.

In general, we are very poor at quantifying risks, and, when asked to do so, begin to flounder. Do you know for example: What is the chance of getting at least one six if a dice is thrown twice? (*See Appendix 1*) What is the chance of being struck by lightning? What is the chance of winning on the Premium Bonds, or on the National Lottery? Is driving on a motorway safer than driving on main roads? Is electricity generation from nuclear power safer and more environmentally friendly than from coal? Is it safer to go caving than to go climbing, or motor-cycling?

Most of the world's problems are clouded in uncertainty. "Global Warming", "Bird Flu'", The MMR injection, GM foods, the spread of AIDS, terrorism, natural disasters and wars are just a few examples. However, some things are absolutely certain. *For example*: Pigs cannot fly unaided. London is in the South of England. The moon orbits the Earth. We shall all die some day. We journey through the uncertainty of life to the certainty of death, navigating to the end by experience and the faith that we have about the way that the universe works.

Scientists and mathematicians have developed statistics to handle uncertainty. Statistics is based on the science of probability and was developed to analyze quantitative data taken from '*populations*', or from well-controlled experiments. Using statistical analysis, hypotheses, or models of reality, can be rigorously tested and their validity expressed as a quantified probability or '*Degree of Confidence*'. Most scientists will accept a hypothesis if it has a probability of only one in a hundred of being incorrect (*or 99% Confidence in their vernacular*). Of course this does not mean that the hypothesis is absolutely correct. Some may not accept a hypothesis unless there is a one in a thousand chance of it being incorrect (99.9% *Confidence level*). Unfortunately, to achieve such high levels of confidence usually requires so much accurate data that the experiments would take forever! This problem applies to the latest 'Theory of Everything' based on a '*String Theory*' that cannot be tested. Scientists argue among themselves about this as a matter of belief! Engineers, being practical, have to balance risk and cost and often use a probability of one in twenty (*95% Confidence*) to design and construct equipment. It is clear that scientists and technologists have to put their faith in statisticians and their chosen level of confidence! Therefore it is not surprising that most advances in science and technology are based initially on faith. This applies especially to unexpected changes and developments that challenge existing frameworks of scientific belief. Uncertainty is the point where faith and science meet.

The framework of beliefs that is accepted in a community, or its '*World View*', is nowadays termed a '*Paradigm*'. Scientists speak of a '*Paradigm Shift*' taking place when old hypotheses are abandoned for new ones. A paradigm shift occurred when Copernicus postulated that the Earth orbited the sun, also when Einstein discarded Newton's concept of 'Absolute Space', for that of 'Relativity'. Darwin's theory of evolution caused another paradigm shift, as did the discovery of the structure of DNA.

Paradigm shifts are not restricted to science, but can occur in society. Karl Marx caused a paradigm shift when he launched the ideology of communism. Tom Paine also caused a paradigm shift in society, as did Christ, Buddha, and other teachers. In recent years, '*relativism*' has shaken society and the demand for 'Rights' has overwhelmed the responsibility for 'Duties'. The enormous increase in the speed and complexity of global communications and information handling has also changed society. Whatever caused it, there has been a paradigm shift in the values of Western Society. As a consequence, the general public has lost confidence in both science and religion to answer questions about uncertainty. Risk aversion, disrespect for authority, litigation and moral bankruptcy are now endemic in the western world.

In the search for knowledge about the universe, scientists and philosophers ask different questions. Scientists ask the question "How?" Philosophers ask the question "Why?" Whilst scientists use logic and repeatable experiments to justify their hypotheses, religious folk use intuition, direct experience and ancient lore. In the last decades, our understanding of these issues has changed. The deeper scientists probe, the more uncertainty they uncover. The more religious people strive to understand science and apply it to their beliefs, the more they discover about their faith.

The key decisions in life are always made with some uncertainty. We cannot know everything. We have to trust those who profess to know about subjects of which we are ignorant. Consequently, everyone has to trust or believe in something. Primitive people believe in luck and superstitions. The Greeks believed that their gods controlled chance events. Throwing yarrow roots, or coins, is used to identify helpful hexagrams in the ancient 'Book of Changes'; the *I Ching*. The belief in determinism and predestation is a help to some, but does not allow for the gift of free will. Humanists, atheists and other secular people all have their beliefs, albeit faith in their own judgement. Faith is not a cure for uncertainty, however, but a navigational aid. (*My car has a satellite navigation system. I do not know how it works, but how comforting it is, when I am lost in a maze of city streets, to press the 'Home' button and be guided back to where I live!*)

Since human life began, uncertainty has stimulated science and religion in the search for truth. The primitive religions developed as ritualistic attempts to control the uncertainty of natural events for their survival. Weather, warfare and plague have always catalysed religious activity and conversion. Uncertainty is a characteristic of the Universe that humankind cannot fathom. Faith was developed to help us deal with it. Faith is not credulousness, however. Credulousness, the willingness to believe anything however feeble the evidence, is not faith. True faith comes from a source outside us. We particularly recognise faith when we find ourselves believing something reluctantly, in spite of ourselves. For our faith to thrive, we need to nurture it. We need to cultivate a disposition that can sense the music of the Universe and allow our faith to flourish. We need to review and refresh our faith in the light of the continual change and uncertainty to which we are exposed. In this respect, uncertainty keeps us on the ball and is a blessing in disguise!

Older cavers usually have to take greater care than younger ones, as their risks are often higher due to their physical ageing. Older cavers do not have the agility and speed of younger cavers, especially when making 'dynamic moves' across difficult climbs. Older cavers who are taking medicines also have to take care as there are risks involved from side effects. Diclofenac, a non-steroidal anti-inflammatory drug, is very good for alleviating the pain of arthritis, but has side effects that can cause cardio-vascular problems if taken regularly. For myself, I try to control this risk by only taking a few tablets for specific trips of over two hours and do not take the tablets daily. Older cavers also need to decide when to bin their old equipment and clothing. In this instance, economy is not as important as personal safety. All cavers take calculated risks underground. The decision to go underground when the weather is unsettled is a difficult one. On long expeditions, it is often common to use thinner ropes to keep the tackle weight down, but this means that great care must be taken to avoid abrasion. All cavers take spare lighting, first aid kits and enough food and drink to sustain them underground. Ropes are carefully rigged with double belays to halve the risk of an anchor failing. Loose boulders and water levels are watched most carefully to avoid trouble, too.

Like all risky sports, caving can be done safely, but there will always be a certain degree of risk present. There is no such thing as zero risk. Those who enjoy dangerous sports such as caving, mountaineering, canyoning, motorcycling, hang-gliding and horse riding, do so with the dangers in mind. For these people, the risk is worth the benefit of their life-style and even a life on the couch has its risks. So, whether you go caving or not, just think carefully when you feel inclined to take a risk!

8
Lanzarote Lava Tube Caves

The earth shook from the tremendous explosion of a volcanic eruption, deep under the ocean. A brilliant, fiery, jet of molten magma and black ash shot miles high into the air. Gobbets of hot lava, rock and ash rained down. The whole world trembled, from its vomiting throat to its distant poles. A massive tsunami set off across the ocean to assault the far shores of land. The skies darkened around the globe as the eruption continued, exploding in paroxysms of rage for several days. This volcanic action, millions of years ago, from a volcanic hot-spot in the Earth's crust, was part of the process that formed The Canary Islands.

This tremendous volcanic activity gave birth to the island of Lanzarote, one of the last of the Canary Islands to be formed. The last of sporadic volcanic eruptions on Lanzarote occurred about two hundred years ago. Nowadays, the island's volcanoes are all extinct or dormant, but the Lanzarote landscape has an imposing backdrop of extinct volcanoes as a result. The mountainous appearance, on closer inspection, reveals high volcanic cones, each with a ridge around a crater and extensive lava fields. The ridge routes provide some spectacular walking, as well as local colours and impressive scenery. For anyone interested in the fascinating subject of vulcanology, there is an excellent exhibition and tour in the Timanfaya National Park at the South end of the island.

In spite of the lava fields being largely barren, the early peasants, or 'Campesinos', made significant use of them. They used the lava for constructing windbreaks, boundary walls and buildings. They also fertilised and tilled the granular, weather-worn, pumice to cultivate crops in small walled fields. The plant life that ekes out a difficult existence in the old lava fields is very colourful and amazingly abundant in places. There are many beautiful, peaceful, walks and picnic spots to visit as a consequence.

The island economy is heavily dependent on tourism. It is a thriving holiday destination where foreign visitors populate the sandy beaches and coastal resorts, rarely venturing into the hinterlands except on coach tours. Exceptionally good wind-surfing, sailing and diving are popular attractions, too. In spite of the problems in 'The Peninsula', as the islanders call Spain, Lanzarote is a very successful holiday resort. For the caver, there are several extensive and interesting lava cave systems to explore, too.

It is always inspiring to do something different, especially for older cavers who have only caved in limestone caves. The Lanzarote lava tube caves present a marvellous opportunity to cave in a completely different and relatively comfortable environment. Unlike limestone caves, lava tube caves are dry and warm. The major systems have very large passages that are fairly easy to explore, although in some place it is necessary to crawl through boulder piles or smaller tubes. The temperature in the lava tube caves on Lanzarote hovers about fifteen to eighteen degrees Celsius all year round, so specialised clothing is not needed. All in all, a good prospect in which older cavers can have fun.

My first visit to Lanzarote was as a sun-seeking holiday maker. Dilys and I rented a villa in Costa Teguise and hired a car to explore the island. There are many paths and walks on the island and, using a guidebook, I walked up and around the crater of an extinct volcano near our villa and, later, went on to explore many scenic and enjoyable walks in different parts of the island. One day we took the car to explore the North end of the island, as far as the port of Orzola. En route for Orzola, we saw signs for the '*Jameos del Agua*' and '*Cueva de los Verdes*' show caves. The word '*Cueva*' prompted an irresistible urge to make a detour, but we stuck to our original plan and visited the small harbour at the end of the island.

A few days later, we returned to visit the '*Cueva de los Verdes*' and paid for a guided tour. The cave passages were surprisingly large and the well placed, subtle, coloured, lighting gave the passages and caverns a magical quality. In one of the caverns, the guide gathered us together and asked us to quieten down so that we could experience the silence. He told us that the cave had once been used as a refuge by the islanders when marauding pirates came to the island. There was a source of water inside the cave and a secret entrance, through which food could be passed to those inside. In addition, he told us that there was a 'surprise' nearby that we were not to reveal to anyone! Even as an experienced caver, I was taken by surprise, so it is worth a visit if you have not been there. The guide then took us further in to visit another large chamber. Here, we stopped for a lecture on volcanoes, the cave formation and history. While he was speaking, I noticed that there were large boulders blocking the tourist path at the end of the chamber, but it was obvious that the passage continued further into the unlit darkness beyond. I asked the guide how far the passage went. He told us that it went on for a considerable distance and that speleologists had made a connection, through several kilometres of passages, to the *Montana Corona* volcano some miles away. This revelation inspired me to investigate the truth of this information when I returned home.

I discovered that Carmen Smith of The Wessex Cave Club had written a very good guide to the caves of Lanzarote, available as a PDF on the website www.cavesoflanzarote.co.uk. When I contacted her, she was most helpful and enthusiastically encouraged me to visit the caves. Carmen gave me the names and addresses of her local caving contacts; Javier Trujillo Gutierrez and Alexandre Perez Perdoma, chairman and secretary of the '*Grupo de Espeleologia de Canarias*' respectively. Without further ado, I rang Javier up and arranged to meet him on our next visit to Lanzarote the following year.

As usual there were baggage restrictions for the flight out, so I only took a caving helmet, headlamp, a few alloy carabiners and a tape sling. I wore a pair of light walking boots to travel in the plane and carried a small rucksack that would survive underground handling. According to Javier, this would be quite enough for an expedition into the *Montana Corona* lava cave system. As in the previous year, I also took a walking pole in the hope that I could use it to ease my arthritic knee above and below ground.

As soon as we had settled into our villa, I rang Javier and he suggested that we meet him in the foyer of the five star 'Gran Hotel' in Arrecife. Arrecife is the island capital and we had purposely avoided it the year before as we did not want to visit a busy town with lots of traffic and a confusion of one-way streets. When I asked Javier where the Gran Hotel was, he told me that it was un-missable and was surprised that I had never seen it! Unlike all of the low buildings on the island, it was seventeen storeys high and visible from miles away! I soon located it on the map that came with the hire car. The next day, we drove out along the Arrecife '*Circunvalacion*' and found it easily, using line-of-sight navigation. We parked in the underground car-park of the hotel with no problems. It was a short walk to the hotel, where we sat in comfortable armchairs in the foyer to wait for Javier. He arrived in Spanish time, but only a quarter of an hour late. As we had never seen each other before, we examined everyone who came into the hotel, expecting any one of them to be him. When Javier eventually arrived, he was unmistakable! Tall, bronzed and wiry, with jet black hair tied at the back, he was a really striking personality. It was a pleasure to meet him and we were soon talking ten to the dozen, as we introduced ourselves. While we had been waiting, Dilys and I had discovered that there was a café on the top floor, with a panoramic view of the island. Javier told us that it was well worth a visit, so the three of us took the lift up to the seventeenth floor to have coffee together. Dilys was really patient with us as her Spanish was minimal and Javier and I were chattering away at high speed. It was very apparent that Javier was as much of a chatterbox as I was!

On the seventeenth floor, we walked out of the lift, along a passage and into the restaurant. Immediately we were confronted with a fantastic panoramic view, high over the island. We chose a table by one of the floor-to-ceiling windows. Dilys dared not go close to the windows as the drop below was vertiginous, but she admired the palm trees on the sandy beach that ran along the seafront as we waited for our *cortados*. Over coffee, I explained to Javier that our visit to the show cave had prompted my interest in *Montana Corona* and that I would like to explore it further. He suggested that we should go into *Jameo de la Puerta Falsa* as far as the gate to the show cave for starters and then explore the rest for the system a few days later. This seemed an excellent plan to me. We decided to meet up in two days time, when I would pick him up from a large free car-park near the bus station, collect Alexandre at Tahiche and drive us out to the cave together.

At the agreed time, I arrived in the car-park, but, as usual, Javier was on Spanish time, so I had to wait longer than I had expected. We drove to Tahiche and had a coffee as we waited for Alexandre and eventually drove out Los Verdes, where I parked the car in a passing place on the road near *Jameo de la Puerto Falsa*. I put my boots on and we walked along a barely visible footpath, through a lava field dotted with green *Tabaiba* bushes. In a few yards, we came to the edge of an enormous hole, at least twenty metres deep. To the right of this deep hole, I could see the huge entrance of *Puerta Falsa*, the lowest freely accessible entrance into the *Montana Corona* system.

There was a steep, pumice-strewn, path that led to the down-flow entrance, but, as we descended, I could see the up-flow entrance to the left, too. I was most surprised at the size of the entrances, having imagined that lava tubes would be fairly small. However, according to Javier, the up-flow tubes were even bigger and probably the largest in diameter in the world. We put on our helmets, tested our lights, shouldered our rucksacks and Javier led us over the boulders into the down-flow cave. There was a great deal of boulder hopping involved as we followed the passage down-flow towards *La Cueva de los Verdes*. I had been advised to wear shorts, as the atmosphere in the lava tubes was too warm for over-suits or trousers. However, I quickly discovered that the boulder surfaces were very rough and sharp! When I just brushed against one with my shin, I badly grazed myself! I decided that for future trips in lava tubes, I would wear long trousers as the locals did!

Jameo de la Puerta Falsa

March 2011

I was most impressed at the size, silence and dryness of the passages. In some places there were white deposits of gypsum. On the walls and ceilings this gave a white cloud-like appearance in the light of our lamps. The gypsum underfoot looked like snow and floated up as we passed. We were soon well coated with it! As the pumice rocks were very rough and abrasive, climbing the boulders and balconies that were in our way was fairly easy. We continued along the passage, until we came to the gated barrier to the show cave and a sort of underground laboratory. There was a gap to one side that allowed us to climb up and visit the refuge that the islanders had used when pirates came. There was a small supply of water drips there, so they could survive for many weeks with food supplies sent in secretly from above. We did not have permission to exit through the show cave, so had to return the same way as we had come. By the time that we resurfaced, we had been caving for a couple of hours and were quite thirsty. We returned to the car, brushed ourselves down and I drove us back to an al fresco lunch that Dilys had prepared for us. We ate a most refreshing meal together, lubricated by plenty of the local 'Tropical' lager and animated by continuous chatter. Eventually I felt ready for a siesta, but had to ferry Javier and Alexandre home. As we prepared to leave, I thanked them for giving me a most enjoyable and unforgettable first caving trip on Lanzarote. The prospect of many more to come was a promising thought, too!

A few days later, we drove out past 'El Monumento del Campesino', turned right near a chapel at Masdache, drove along the road towards La Vegueta and parked in a dusty lay-by, near a walled garden, to visit *La Cueva de Las Naturalistas*. This cave is called *Las Palomas* by the locals, due to the numerous pigeons that nest in the entrances. Apparently, the *Campesinos* used to breed and catch them, as well as stealing their eggs for food. *La Cueva de Las Naturalistas* was smaller in cross-section than the *Montana Corona* cave and had a hemi-spherical passage shape, with a flat floor. The absence of large boulders and the flat floor made it much easier to negotiate. The lava tube was very near to the surface and small holes let daylight in at one or two places. Javier told me that a local farmer was driving a heavy truck along of the tracks nearby when, to his dismay, it broke into a lava tube underneath! On the surface, Alexandre had shown me lots of interesting holes that must have had potential disaster for tractors, too. At one point further inside *La Cueva de Las Naturalistas*, Alexandre pointed out some small hanging formations like little stalactites. Apparently these were formed by molten lava, dripping down, as the tube emptied out after an eruption. After examining a couple of small, low, side routes, we climbed out to the surface, about half a mile away. This completed another enjoyable morning traverse before lunch. Just the job for an older caver!

The following year, I again caved with Javier, Alexandre and Brahim, another club member, to complete the rest of the *Montana Corona* system. The first trip was into the left-hand entrance of *Puerta Falsa*, traversing up-flow to *Jameo de la Gente*. We descended into the open pit and walked under an overhang, used by local rock climbers. Their fixed anchors and chalky fingerprints could be seen along several vertical and overhanging climbing routes above us. The rocks in the daylight zone were a bright green, giving the place a somewhat unworldly appearance. The traverse took about an hour and was in large passages, with lots of boulder hopping and a single constriction under a large boulder choke, about a third of the way in. The deposits of gypsum powder and concretions on the lower walls were just like snow in many places and reflected the lights of our head-lamps, so that the scene was well illuminated. There were several rounded balconies that we carefully traversed across, high above the passage floor, as a welcome respite from boulder hopping. For the first time ever, I successfully used a walking pole underground to assist my arthritic knees! The final exit was into *Jameo de la Gente*, a large crater that was most impressive and used for picnics by the locals, hence its name. I saw several tomato plants flourishing in the sunlit area, presumably from the pips of jettisoned tomatoes! There was an easy climb up to the surface, just before the up-flow passage to the rest of the system, that led to *Jameo de Prendes*, the top entrance to the system. The best way back to the car would have been to take the road. However, Brahim led us on a 'short cut' over the 'badlands'. It was very rough terrain once we left the vestigial foot path and awfully rugged, hard going. Leaving Brahim to continue to follow his route, the rest of us diverted to the road and easier going. Needless to say Brahim arrived back at the car first, but we were glad not to have sprained an ankle, or to have fallen into a thorn bush.

A few days later, we re-visited *Las Naturalistas* with Carmen, Chris Binding, Aubrey Newport and Noel Cleave from the Wessex Cave Club, who had come out for a week's caving. They went caving every day and suggested several future trips that I would enjoy. In the evenings, we met in the local tapas bar and shared bottles of wine together. Aubrey and Noel returned home at the end of that week, but Chris and Carmen stayed on for two days afterwards. They subsequently helped with the logistics of my next caving trip.

At the weekend, Javier, Alexandre, Brahim and I completed the rest of the *Montana Corona* system by traversing underground from *Jameo de la Gente* to *Jameo de Prendes*. I was particularly grateful when Chris volunteered to drive us back to recover my hire car, parked by the *Jameo de La Gente* entrance, some kilometres away, after we had completed the traverse and emerged from *Jameo de Prendes.*

The traverse took us about three hours and was the best part of the *Montana Corona* system in my opinion. The climb down into the up-flow passages of *Jameo de la Gente* was easy. A scramble over greenish rocks led to a wooden ladder that had a rung missing at the bottom. From here on up-flow, the passages were very high, wide and silently enormous. White gypsum powder decorated the walls, ceilings and floors in several places to give a less sombre atmosphere than that in the darker passages. The going was quite strenuous, with lots of boulder piles to climb, several traverses along walls and balconies, and a short, low, crawl that led to lava tubes on two levels. My walking pole was really useful as we crossed the rocks, as it not only rested my knees, but enabled me to balance when I had to step across the wider gaps in the rocks. Eventually, the route led via an upwards scramble over boulders to a short 7m pitch, where we stopped to take a snack and a drink.

Steel ring-bolts were fixed in place at the top of the pitch. Javier used these to attach a pull-through rope for our descent. Javier and Brahim soon had the pitch rigged and Alexandre descended first, with me following. The descent was fairly easy, even though I was using an unfamiliar descender that Javier had lent me. I had left my faithful rack at home to keep within my baggage allowance on the flight out. The only problem was that the top of the pitch started over a bulge and from there it was free-hanging to the floor. Kneeling against the slope using my knee-pads worked well when I could not locate the two hidden footholds that Javier had described below the bulge. When we had all descended, Javier pulled the rope down with no problems and we continued up-flow. The way on was upwards over more large, rough boulders, until we came to a large chamber with a 25m vertical climb. Javier free-climbed this and fixed a rope for the rest of us to climb using hand-jammers. Near the top, there was a small hole to squeeze through. Because I did not need it, I had collapsed my walking pole and packed it into my rucksack, with the point sticking up behind me. Needless to say, as I squeezed through the hole, this jammed against the top of the hole! I had to back out, taking care not to fall down the climb, take off the rucksack and pass it to Javier before I could get through. Alexandre and Brahim ascended without incident and Javier undid the rope, packed it into his tackle bag and set off towards the entrance. From the top of the pitch, it was only a short distance to the entrance. We passed across a large, deep, hole by traversing on the right-hand wall, using small cracks and a useful, roughly surfaced, handhold, to enter the final chamber. Here, Chris was waiting for us, just at the end of the daylight zone. He had kindly agreed to ferry us back downhill to our car and asked what we had just been doing. He could hear our shouted conversations, but as they were in Spanish he did not know what was happening!

Once we were in the daylight zone, I saw that the exit was in another large crater. We climbed up the wall of this, for a height of several metres, then inched our way along a ledge to a metal gate on the surface. Chris had parked the car at the end of the dusty track from the cave, so we did not have to walk far. Carmen and her aunt Joyce were also there to greet us. We were soon changed and the gear all packed into the boot. Chris drove us back to my car and then we went in convoy back to the villa, where Dilys had another delicious al fresco lunch ready for us. A convivial lunch with plenty of '*Tropical*' lager ended another most enjoyable and unforgettable morning caving.

The following year, I had another very interesting expedition with Javier into *La Cueva del Paso o del Esqueleto*, not far from the coastal footpath that runs Northwards from the village of El Golfo. The cave is difficult to find and has a very small entrance. After half an hour's walk along the scenic coastal path, with waves crashing on the rocks in the bright sunshine, we detoured into one of the '*islotes*' of old lava that had not been covered by the eruptions in the 1700's that formed the Timanfaya National Park. Javier explained that there were basically two types of lava in the park, named after similar lavas in Hawaii. The main lava fields that we had been walking through were of a rocky, rough, lava called '*A'aā*' lava. The lava in the '*islote*' that we had just reached, was of smooth, unbroken, lava called *Pāhoehoe* lava. It was fortunate that we were able to walk on the *Pāhoehoe* lava as the '*A'aā* lava would have been utterly impassable on foot!

It took some to time to find the entrance, but was well worth it. The initial constriction went to the top of a steep climb down into a large passage. Luckily, the roughness of the pumice made for easy hand and footholds. Javier let me lead the way on to get the best impression of the cave. In my opinion, *Esqueleto* is one of the most interesting and beautiful of the Lanzarote caves. It has large bands and drifts of powdered gypsum that make it rather dusty in places, but the black ceilings with their white calcite and gypsum concretions running along the cracks, provide a superb contrast to the snow-like floors. At one point, Javier told me to stop and turn off my light. Once we were in pitch darkness, it was possible to see, high above us, a bright spark of sunlight, coming through a tiny hole in the roof. Lava tubes, formed as the molten lava solidifies, often have thin parts of the roof quite near the surface. The large passage soon deteriorated to a low crawl, where I was glad of my knee-pads. The crawl continued for some distance, until it opened out into a larger passage again. Throughout the cave there was a steady breeze, refreshingly cool and damp. As I emerged from the crawl, the breeze seemed stronger and smelt of the sea. The reason for this soon became apparent. The cave ended in a cliff over the sea! There was a fantastic view ahead! I crossed a flat floor, spotted with bird droppings, to the brightly lit opening above the Atlantic. Below the lip of the entrance, the waves were crashing on the rocks, with clouds of white sparkling spray. The whole effect was really dazzling to my eyes after the unremitting darkness of the cave. Javier and I spent some time at our ease there, enjoying the superb view. Seated in comfort on flat pumice, we first satisfied our thirsts from our water bottles, then consumed some delicious 'gofio', a local sort of parkin made from maize flour. 'Gofio' is a very good energy source as it contains fourteen different ingredients, including fruits and nuts. It is also very tasty and we ate it all up!

The journey out to the surface, once our eyes had accommodated to the darkness again, was surprisingly quick. Crawls are often quicker on the return than on the way out for some reason. The beautiful scenery of the cave was still sufficient to make us pause occasionally to admire it, even so. The walk back to the car also seemed to be shorter and it was not long before we were back at the villa in Costa Teguise and enjoying another superb lunch that Dilys had prepared for us, with lots of 'Tropical' lager to drink. Yet another really enjoyable caving trip to savour in later times!

There are lots of other interesting lava tube caves to visit on the island, one with a hundred metre deep pitch for the SRT enthusiasts. The advantage that Lanzarote offers older cavers with arthritis, particularly in the winter months, is that the warm climate seems to loosen up the joints. It could very well be the effects of more wine and 'Tropical' than usual, but warm sun can do wonders. The sun is also an excuse to do nothing except sun-bathe! Older people often have a Vitamin D deficiency that can be alleviated by exposure to sunshine, so if in doubt then lie in the sun for a while. The other Canary Islands are all volcanic and have lava tube caves, too. So, all in all, there is no need for older cavers to endure the damp and chilly British weather if they can take a holiday in the sundrenched Canaries and explore lava tube caves, too!

9
Moving Targets

Anyone can dream. Many people dream of winning the lottery. Bankers dream of making money. Politicians dream of power. Engineers dream of perfect systems. Artists dream of beautiful forms and colours. Mystics dream of enlightenment. Athletes dream of winning an Olympic Gold medal. Mountaineers dream of climbing to the top of Everest. Cavers dream of discovering caverns that are deep, long and beautiful.

Dreaming is a particular activity for older people when they cannot perform as well as they could when they were younger. Ambitions have to be pruned with old age and there are few exceptions. Childhood dreams are usually abandoned during adult life. A few people, who are gifted with superb mental and physical fitness in old age, can still realise their ambitions past the age of seventy. The celebrity adventurer Sir Ranulph Fiennes climbed Everest when he was sixty-five and planned to cross the Antarctic in winter at sixty eight, but his trip had to be aborted when one of his fingers was badly frost-bitten. It will be very interesting to see what he does when he is over seventy! The famous French caver Norbert Casteret caved in the Pierre Saint Martin when he was sixty and lived until the age of ninety. Most of us ordinary people have to pick targets within the constraints that our genes or life-style have set for us. Older cavers are no exception, but there are plenty of dreams for them to enjoy and realise. The deepest, the longest, the most beautiful and the most wonderful caves are all there in the real world. The problem for older cavers is that they may be inaccessible. Ageing is unavoidable, so our dreams and ambitions have to be aimed at continuingly moving targets.

In the working world, people aim for targets that are 'SMART'. This acronym can be interpreted in several different ways, but for older cavers it stands for S=Specific, M=Meaningful, A=Attainable, R=Relevant and T=Timed. This interpretation is useful for assessing dreams and targets in the world of caving and potholing. Cavers aim for specific challenges, the most common being a new discovery or depth record. The length of a cave system will usually include all of the side passages, so a specific target would be to traverse such a system between two entrances. An example of such a target would be to traverse the Pierre Saint Martin from the Tête Sauvage to the EDF tunnel in the Pyrenees. Some caves are very beautiful and present a specific target to be visited for photography or simple wonder. It is not easy to decide which cave is the most beautiful in the world, but most cavers would probably choose Lechuguilla in New Mexico. Lechuguilla is also the seventh longest in the world.

Caving expeditions are meaningful in different ways for each of the cavers who are making them. For example, the leader may not be so interested in getting to the bottom of a deep cave as in getting the expedition members safely back to the surface. Older cavers cave for different reasons from younger cavers because they have restrictions on what is physically attainable and may value comfort and physical enjoyment more than depth or length. Cavers would argue that they aim for a relevant new experience when they enter a cave system. The exception might be visits to show caves. "Cave Tourism" is one of the most derogatory descriptions that can be applied to an expedition into a known cave, even if the cavers are leading and entering the system for the first time. In fact, the use of the word 'Tourist' in an unfriendly or derogatory manner is usually a sign of resentment or xenophobia above or below ground!

For older cavers, the length or timing of some expeditions has to constrained, especially if they lack the stamina of their youth. Hardened cavers, especially young machos, sometimes aim to complete an expedition as fast as possible, aiming to set a record for reaching a specific depth or for traversing a specific length. This sort of target would probably not be meaningful to the majority of cavers and, in fact, such competitions organised for commercial gain are abhorrent. A few examples of the sort of targets that attract, or are dreamt of, by cavers are given in the following paragraphs, beginning with depth:

Krubera, a cave in the Arabika massif, high in the Western Caucasus, is the deepest known cave in the world. The entrance was discovered in 1960 and explored as far as an impassable squeeze. Subsequently, the Kiev Speleological Club began work in the cave in 1980, widening squeezes and exploring to a depth of -340m. The cave has several side passages and sumps at various depths, and exploration has been by diving sumps and discovering new passages. 'Sump 1' at -1,440m. is free-diveable, but presents a significant psychological barrier to be passed. At the end of the last millennium, further explorations extended it deeper and deeper; to pass the -2000m depth in 2004 in a new section of cave called 'Windows'. In 2010, the 'Two Captains' sump was dived to -2,140m. In 2012, an expedition was launched for divers to push even deeper and a record of -2197m was achieved during a dive in the 'Terminal Sump'. The length of the cave was then 16,098m. An expedition to the bottom of this cave is the dream of any able-bodied caver. Older cavers can only dream of actually going there, but they can cave vicariously through the expedition reports, stories and articles in magazines.

Mammoth Cave in Kentucky, with about 628 kilometres of passages, is the longest in the world. However, there are many traverses elsewhere of considerable length and beauty that can be chosen for specific targets and every caver will have a favourite. Mine was the Sima Cueto to Coventosa traverse in Spain, which I completed when I was younger. Nowadays I have to make do with Thistle cave at Ribblehead!

Lechuguilla, in New Mexico, is widely considered to be the most beautiful cave in the world and access is restricted to keep it that way. This means that only a chosen few can visit the cave and the rest of us have to be content with the superb photographs and videos that are available. However, it is not only speleo-thems, crystals, limpid pools and stream-ways that are beautiful. There are the petroglyphs of early man and the cave paintings of the Magdalenian era. As well as beauty, cave paintings have a magic about them that defies description. Again, to conserve them, access is restricted and we can only see them as photographs or realistic copies. Cave conservation is essential to preserve such valuable items. In caves where access is not controlled, the cavers visiting them need to be well-educated in cave conservation so that they do not inadvertently cause any damage.

Depth, length and beauty are only three attributes of caving systems. There are many other attributes that cavers consider when they are deciding which cave system to visit. For the toughest and most adventurous cavers, the severity of the cave is important. The severity is governed by the obstacles encountered such as the length of the cave, the number of deep shafts, tight squeezes, difficult climbs, deep water and passages full of water with a tiny airspace, or sumps. For older cavers, the severity of a cave system requires serious consideration. Some of the most severe systems are for young, very fit and thin cavers only!

Another attribute of a cave is its distance from the caver's home. Nowadays, cavers travel all over the world and there are many expeditions to China, Vietnam, Russia, Albania and other remote and previously inaccessible places. The older caver will probably be restricted to Europe, or to countries where medical cover is at an acceptable price. Besides, it is very pleasant to take one's grandchildren caving near home!

Accessibility is another important cave attribute. Some caves are so beautiful, or have such rare fauna, that access is restricted to conserve them. Lechuguilla and the painted cave of Altemira are only two examples of this aspect. Entry is strictly controlled to prevent any destruction of the cave's beauty and environment. Even with authorisation, cavers have to take great care not to leave any biological debris or to damage anything accidentally. Many popular caves have had their formations and fauna destroyed by the passage of too many careless cavers.

For anyone with a mathematical and logical turn of mind, it is possible to rank caves against several attributes using weighting methods, or specialised decision analysis software. Older cavers cannot be bothered with such technology and just use their common sense! In any case, the attributes and alternatives change as one's age increases....

Older cavers are always aiming at moving targets!

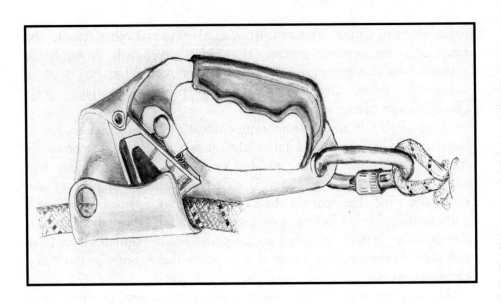

10
Up the Aranzadi Wall

The Pierre Saint Martin cave system, in the Western Pyrenees, has a long and interesting history of exploration. The system was discovered in 1950 by Georges Lépineux and Guiseppe Occhialini, who saw a jackdaw fly out of a hole in the limestone near the frontier-stone Pierre Saint Martin. They dropped stones down the hole, concluded that it must be very deep indeed and informed the caving community at that time. The first descent was made in 1951, using a winch to lower cavers down the shaft. The Lépineux shaft, as it was named, proved to be 320m. (1050ft.) deep. In 1952, an expedition led by Max Cosyns, explored from the bottom of the shaft as far as 'The Metro', a huge gallery deep in the system. The caverns and passages in the PSM are really enormous. Some of the blocks on the floor are so large that people have lost their way going around them! The Cosyns team also used an electric winch on the entrance shaft, but the expedition was curtailed due to a fatal accident. Tragically, Marcel Loubens, a popular member of the team, fell to his death when his attachment to the cable failed. A special project was organised to remove his body in 1954 and the chamber at the bottom of the shaft named in his memory.

In 1953, the caverns and passages at the bottom of the shaft were explored through three kilometres of passages to the enormous 'La

Verna' chamber at a depth of 734m. This was a world depth record at that time! 'La Verna' was surveyed and found to be 250 metres in diameter and 190 metres high. The volume of the chamber was 3.6 Million cubic metres with a surface area of five hectares. It was the largest underground chamber in the world at that time, too.

Teams of speleologists conducted many research studies in the system, as well as exploration. Hydrological studies of the system were carried out for the French company Electricité de France (EDF). As a result of these studies, in the late '50s, EDF drove a tunnel into 'La Verna' in search of a source of hydro-electric power. However, they drove the tunnel too high to be of use and it was abandoned. Fortunately for cavers, it eventually enabled 'through trips' from the plateau above. Exploration continued apace and in 1962, the 80m. high 'Aranzadi Wall' in 'La Verna' was climbed to enter a large passage that led to the 'Meander Martine'. Further exploration past the meander achieved a depth of 1006m. in 1965. At the same time, several teams were looking for caves in the limestone massif above and the Tête Sauvage pothole was discovered. In 1966, the Tête Sauvage pothole was connected to the PSM system. This resulted in an overall depth of 1171m. and set a new depth record.

With a huge system of caves and potholes to explore in the massif, the cavers formed ARSIP, (L'Association pour la Recherche Spéléologique Internationale á la Pierre Saint Martin) to conserve, coordinate and record explorations in the system. During the 60's and 70's, several entrances to the system were discovered in the limestone plateau and, at the same time, further underground discoveries increased the length of the system. In 1975, following the discovery of the SC3 entrance in the plateau, the depth record increased to 1321m. In 1981, the Pourtet pothole was discovered and connected to the PSM. The system is currently the 17th. deepest in the world, with a depth of 1342m. between the Pourtet entrance and the bottom of the 'Aziza-Parment' pitch at the end of the system, reached via the 'Aranzadi Wall'. With about 50 kilometres of passages and caverns, the PSM is the 45th longest in the world and is a veritable magnet for cavers from all over the world.

When I was in the sixth form at school, I read about the recovery of Marcel Louben's body in a book by Jacques Attout, the expedition chaplain. The epic story inspired me to take up potholing later in life. However, I never realised then that I would visit 'La Salle Loubens' myself, nor that I would visit the Pierre Saint-Martin several times and complete the Tête Sauvage to EDF tunnel traverse! In the visits of my later life, I was always impressed by the gigantic size of the PSM caverns and passages and particularly at the vast chamber of 'La Verna'. I knew about the system at the top of the 'Aranzadi Wall', too. Nevertheless, since the 80m. climb up the 'Aranzadi Wall' looked so intimidating after a hard caving trip, I was never tempted to climb it and visit the caverns beyond. There is always a finite limit to one's strength and stamina!

Imagine my amazement, when in my seventies, I was asked to do some translation work for leaflets and guides to 'La Verna' and discovered that it was going to become a show-cave! Three local communities around the village of Sainte-Engrâce had invested capital in local tourism. They built a reception centre, offices and a car park in the village, opened up a track to the EDF tunnel to take 4x4 minibuses, constructed a new cabin with a toilet, provided a flat concrete path along the EDF tunnel to take wheel-chairs, constructed a viewing platform, installed a spot-light and fitted subtle lighting around 'La Verna' chamber. Nowadays, instead of the arduous struggle up the footpath to the EDF tunnel, you can pay to ride up in a *camionette* and, for a fee, have guided tours of varying difficulty within the PSM. Useful information about costs and booking a visit, can be found on the website www.laverna.fr (*Click on the Union Jack for English*)

The 'La Verna' cavern was once the largest in the world and is still in the top ten for size. It is unbelievably impressive and near the bottom of the Pierre Saint-Martin system. The depth quoted for the PSM is from the highest entrance, to the bottom of the 'Aziza-Parment' pitch that is reached by climbing the 'Aranzadi Wall' in 'La Verna', following the 'Aranzadi Gallery' to the 'Meander Martine' and descending a series of wet pitches and passages that terminate in an impassably tight rift at the bottom of the 'Aziza- Parment' pitch.

Since I helped with the English translations, I was given a free guided trip up the 'Aranzadi Wall' as an *'Accompagnateur'* to a group of local hill walkers. I joined the group with my old friend Michel Lauga, who was one of the two guides that morning, at the tourist centre in Saint-Engrâce. Cedric, the leading guide gave a brief explanation of the visit and the precautions to be taken. He told us that the 80m. free climb on the 'Aranzadi Wall' had a fixed 11mm. rope in place, with three bolt changes. The paying members of the group were provided with strong waterproof overalls, sit-harnesses, *'cow's-tails'*, ascenders and Petzl descenders. Michel and I had our own clothing and equipment. My ancient rack descender and hand-jammer ascender were a considerable source of interest in comparison!

Cedric drove us up-hill in a sturdy mini-bus, along a steep track, bumpy in places and with precipitous drops to one side. We soon arrived at the new cabin near the EDF tunnel and alighted to complete our clothing and equipment adjustments. Cedric gave us a presentation about our route and about the PSM system, using a large survey map on the wall. Then we entered the EDF tunnel in single file and walked to the 'La Verna' viewing platform. The last time that I had walked through the tunnel, it was dark, with a rough and sometimes watery floor. Now the floor had been concreted so that wheel-chairs could be pushed along it and electric lights at intervals lit the path adequately. We re-grouped on the viewing platform and Cedric pointed out the 'Aranzadi Wall' on the other side of the chamber, using a powerful spotlight. It looked very far away! I was very impressed that 'La Verna' was beautifully illuminated to reveal its grandeur. Then it was time to start caving.

We followed Cedric down the boulders and steep, slithery slopes in the vast chamber, to the stream-way. We crossed this, then traversed and climbed towards the base of the 'Aranzadi Wall'. With the new fixed lighting in the chamber, it seemed as if we were out in the open on the side of a mountain. All of the rest of the party were much younger than me and I had some difficulty keeping up with them. I usually had walking poles to aid my arthritic knees when walking on hills like these! I was glad to arrive at the base of the wall and join the group, assembled for Cedric to tell us how to climb the wall. He gave each of us an elastic band and showed us how to fix it around the wrist and then loop it into the ascender that was attached by a safety cord to the sit-harness. Once we were on the wall, the ascender then ran up the rope as we climbed using hands and feet. We were told not to pull on the rope and to keep as close together as possible to avoid stone-falls. I followed the last man of the group, with Michel bringing up the rear behind me. The climb was fairly easy, with only one or two sections having delicate holds. We followed the vertical line of a small water channel that ran down the face. Generally we kept to the right of this, but I found that the best holds were often in the water. The bolt changes were at small ledges and the last section was up a steep muddy slope, where I just ran the carabiners of my 'cow'- tails' along the rope, using it as a hand-line. Needless to say, with 'La Verna' illuminated deep below, the view was quite exciting!

We gathered at the top for photos to be taken. Looking across the vast chamber, we could just make out a group of people on the viewing platform on the other side. How tiny their figures looked at that distance! They could see our lights and shouted to us, their voices deadened by the enormous gap between us. Michel and I looked at our watches and estimated that Dilys and Annie, our wives, were in that group. They had come on a separate trip for non-cavers, some time later that morning. We shouted back, but could not tell if they heard us, so we flashed our lights at them as well. Having established contact, we walked into the 'Aranzadi Gallery'. This was fairly easy going and mainly dry. We climbed down to a small stream after a while, where there were some good formations. The gallery continued, large and impressive, but not as large as the other PSM galleries such as the 'Metro'. The photographers in the group stopped several times to take photos as we came to various small climbs and interesting traverses. In this way, we continued as far as the 'Meander Martine'. Here, we stopped for lunch. Whilst everyone was unpacking, taking photos and so on, I went a short way along the meander. It was fairly easy traversing on jagged holds and I squeezed past some of the narrow sections until I came to what looked like a short pitch, where I turned back. When I returned, the group were all sitting comfortably, with their knapsacks open, munching baguettes and sipping from plastic cups. Like most French walking groups, they had wine. Michel, who had arranged my trip, had provided us both with a very substantial lunch, so the time occupied with eating was longer than expected! Cedric eventually called a halt and we began our return. My knees were a bit stiff and so I welcomed the movement. We were soon at the top of the 'Aranzadi Wall' again.

Cedric and Michel checked that everyone had their descenders ready and then Michel started down the rope first. Once he was at the top belay point, he shouted and I followed him down. I joined him on a capacious sloping surface and discussed the order of descent. Michel stopped at the first bolt change to help the others and I continued down on my own. The muddy 11mm. rope was a bit tight for my rack, so my descent was not as rapid as usual, but very safe! Anyway, I was glad to take my time and stop occasionally to gaze at some really impressive sights in the vastness of 'La Verna'. At the bottom, I waited under an overhang as the others came down, with the occasional stone rattling and crashing ahead of them.

Once everyone was down, Cedric led us down to the bottom of 'La Verna'. From the stance at the base of the 'Aranzadi Wall', we scrambled over the boulders and down steep slopes to the pebble beach at the bottom of 'La Verna'. Cedric pointed out the initials of the first explorers and helped us to look for the rare insects that live there. They seemed to be well hidden, presumably sensing our footfalls, but we did see a couple. They were surprisingly smaller than I had imagined them to be from the photographs in some of the books and journals that I had read. Eventually we climbed up the rocky slope, back to the viewing platform, with Michel and me at the rear. Cedric's idea of returning to the platform '*doucement*' certainly had me '*au bout de souffle*' at the top! An easy walk along the EDF tunnel, with the wind behind us, led us back into the hot sunshine.

We all tidied our gear and clothing and then Cedric drove us back to the village in the minibus. Michel and I changed into our normal clothes by his car and then he drove us back to his house for a meal. Annie and Dilys were waiting for us, with aperitifs and canapés, on the balcony overlooking the Pyrenees. As we sat and sipped our drinks, we exchanged accounts of our respective visits to 'La Verna'. How quickly the day had passed! We raised our glasses to future trips that would be as good as the day's experience. It was a most enjoyable and companionable caving trip for all of us. I was so glad to have been able to experience such an excellent opportunity and that Dilys had seen 'La Verna' at last. It certainly proved that older cavers can still have some fun!

11
Cave Water

Water is essential for life as we know it. The survival of humanity depends primarily on water and wars have been fought over access to it. Our bodies have a hundred times as many water molecules in them as all of the other molecules in the body taken together. Although our planet is a watery one, with almost three-quarters of its surface covered in water, most of the water is in the oceans. Only a fortieth of the world's water is present as fresh water in ice and groundwater. Glaciers, rivers, rain and frost have shaped the landscapes of our world. The continuous cycle of evaporation, transpiration, condensation and precipitation of water in the Earth's atmosphere shapes the weather and harnesses the energy of the Sun. Water is a precious and extraordinary substance that most people take for granted until they are thirsty.

Water has an incredibly wide range of physical and chemical attributes. Physically, depending on the temperature and pressure of its environment, water can exist as a liquid, a solid (*Ice, snow or hail*) and as a gas (*Steam or water vapour*). The chemistry of water has been well researched, but the findings may seem esoteric to the layman. Although the molecular structure of water, with two hydrogen atoms bound to an oxygen atom, may seem simple, the properties of this molecule at the molecular, microscopic and macroscopic levels are not easily explained without knowledge of chemistry and physics. The wonderful range of the chemical and physical properties of water is too deep a subject for this book, but some of the key facts are needed to explain cave formation and decoration.

Water is a very good solvent for many chemical compounds. Water that pours down as rain and flows over moorland, takes up carbon dioxide from the air and peaty surfaces to become acidic. This acidity is sufficient to dissolve limestone and eventually to form cavities, which subsequently develop into caves and potholes, as the water percolates along the beds and joints of the limestone. Water as a solvent is the prime vehicle for the formation of beautiful cave formations such as stalactites, stalagmites, flowstone, cave pearls and crystals. The action of water currents in underground stream-ways is also sufficient to cause abrasion and erosion, particularly if the current is strong enough to convey grit, small pebbles and even boulders. Insoluble residues and entrained particles may settle out of stagnant water to form mud deposits.

Cavers recognise two basic types of cave passage formation. The passages formed under the water-table by solution are termed 'Phreatic'. Those formed by erosion above the water-table are termed 'Vadose'. Speleologists still dispute which of these two types of formation is the most important in cave formation in particular areas. Most cavers just observe the wonders of their effects and do not argue about the theory. It is interesting to note that T-shaped passages are formed by a combination of these two actions, with the horizontal plane caused primarily by phreatic action and the vertical groove below, by later vadose action.

Water is encountered in caves in many different states, several of which contribute to the beauty of the underground scene. Basically, water is either flowing, or static, in a cave. Flowing water is encountered in stream-ways and may be shallow, or deep, depending on the flow-rate and passage size. Water flowing over rocks as a cascade, or hurtling around a bend in the passage, can be quite spectacular. Water flowing over a deep drop as a waterfall can provide a roaring white beauty of its own, too. Water dripping from the roof, or pouring in from an overhead crevice, can provide curtains, or misty atmospheres, as well as a wetting to the caver underneath. If the water contains calcium carbonate in solution and drips slowly, it may form stalactites or curtains that hang from the roof of the cave. Depending on the flow and solute concentration of the drips, they may form stalagmites on the cave floor where they land. Water laden with calcium carbonate that flows slowly over rocky surfaces can deposit a layer of calcite as 'flowstone'. Flowstone deposits of different shapes and quantities provide delightful decorations in cave passages and grottoes. Sometimes the water flowing over flowstone can have iron, or other elements, dissolved in it to produce a coloured flowstone. Small drips of solute laden water in secluded places can also form 'cave pearls', tiny spheroids of calcite crystal, that look just like pearls when they are in the water of their formation.

Static water underground is encountered in lakes, canals, deep pools, puddles, low ducks, sumps or siphons, gour-pools, and as condensation on walls and ceilings. The water in static pools is sometimes coloured green, or blue, depending on the type of solute or colloidal suspension in the water. Condensation droplets en masse on the roof of a cave can provide a display of diamonds in the sky when illuminated by caving head-lamps. Gour-pools, or rim-stone pools are formed when water, containing a high concentration of dissolved compounds in it, trickles over a ledge, or sill, to deposit tiny crystals that act like a dam. Over the years, the crystals build up into an impermeable wall that contains a pool rich in solute. This solute can subsequently form exquisite crystals under the surface. Sometimes gour-pools form in tiers, one above the other, to provide a beautiful crystalline vista, linked by flowstone to look like a hillside terrace, or an exotically stepped pyramid.

Water is so important in the formation and development of cave systems that, when it stops flowing in a passage, that part of the cave system stops developing and is often termed 'fossilised'. Dry, or 'fossilised', passages and caverns often seem lifeless in comparison with passages containing water. They can, nevertheless, be beautifully decorated with Gypsum, Selenite, or other crystals, deposited from films of water containing their salts in solution. Such passages do have a charm of their own, however; silence.

Cavers never take water for granted. Water formed and is still forming, the limestone caves that they explore and enjoy for recreation and scientific research. However, water is the greatest hazard in caves when it rises quickly, or flows in flood, and has caused many caving fatalities. An experienced caver will always check the weather forecast before going underground and keep an eye and ear on the water in an underground stream-way as well as looking for the signs of flooding on the cave walls. It is important to remember that although water is essential for life, it can also be a cause of death from drowning.

12
Wormhole

Once upon a time, a young prince was riding deep in the forest when he noticed a cave entrance at the base of a small rock-face some distance from the path. On an impulse, he dismounted, tethered his horse to a tree and walked over to examine the entrance. In those days, caves were places of mystery and often believed to be the haunt of goblins and giants. He did not believe such stories himself and wondered if the cave would make a good refuge in difficult times. The cave was quite easy to enter and he explored as far as he could see in the daylight filtering in from the entrance. The cave was quite large and dry and would make a good refuge some day. It seemed to continue, but, without a light, he could go no further and had to return to the entrance. The next day, he returned with a pitch torch and some candles to explore further.

The main passage of the cave was quite high and almost circular in cross-section. The cave floor was littered with large boulders that made progress slow, but he managed to climb over and around them, nevertheless. The cave continued straight ahead for several hundred yards, until he was stopped by a huge boulder pile that filled the passage right up to the roof. He climbed to the top of this and searched for a way on. In one place, near the wall, the smoke from his torch was pulled by a slight draught that went down a narrow crack between the rocks. He put his torch down and pulled several small rocks from around the spot where the draught was coming from to uncover a wide gap between the boulders. At this point he hesitated, afraid that he might become trapped if the rocks moved when he was in between them. Eventually, he plucked up enough courage to crawl through the gaps between the boulders, still holding his torch. He eventually emerged at the top of a descending boulder slope in the same circular passage. Peering into the darkness ahead, he could see that the passage stretched far into the distance in a straight line, still circular in shape and of the same dimensions, but with fewer rocks on the floor. He lit a candle and left it near the hole that he had come through to mark his way back. Then he descended the boulder pile and strode off along the passage, making good progress as the floor was clear of obstructions. He walked for at least ten minutes until he could see a curious, silent, blackness filling the passage ahead. Thinking that it was just a large chamber or abyss, he moved carefully towards it. The flickering light from his torch did not penetrate or reflect from it as he approached and he could not see what was ahead at all. The blackness did not reflect the light from his flaming torch. It seemed to be some sort of absorbent cloud, or foggy wall. At this point, he suddenly felt quite scared, never having seen such a phenomenon before. The belief in goblins and giants that he had rejected in the day-light seemed to have more meaning here! He walked up closer to touch it with his torch, but the blackness was not solid and the torch sank into it with no resistance. It seemed to be a sort of curtain, or membrane that stretched from floor to ceiling. He pulled a dagger from his belt and pushed it into the black curtain. There seemed to be a pull on the dagger, so he quickly withdrew it. The dagger seemed to make no cuts in the black curtain when he sliced from side to side with it. The curtain re-sealed as fast as he could cut it. He took his riding crop from his haversack and pushed that into the blackness. Again, there was a significant pull on the riding crop that seemed to get stronger as he pushed it further in. He picked up a rock and threw it in, but it disappeared without a sound. He realised that if he wanted to continue his exploration, he would have to pass through the black curtain. After some hesitation, he put his hand through it, but could feel nothing except the inward pull. When he withdrew his hand, it was unharmed. He had a rope with him, so he threaded it through a small hole in the wall as a belay and tied it around his waist. Then summoning up all of his courage, he stepped forward and walked straight across the threshold.

He felt as if he was falling forwards in pitch darkness! Although he felt that he was falling forwards, he was not falling as fast as he would have if he had fallen down a cliff. He seemed to be sinking into a thick, treacly, blackness. The rope became taut and his falling sensation stopped. He could neither see, nor hear anything in the blackness, except for the sputtering of his flaming torch. Scared stiff, he pulled on the rope and managed to get back over the threshold and into the cave again. The black curtain re-sealed behind him and he was unharmed. He decided to get away from there as quickly as he could before his torch burnt out. As he retraced his steps, he began to wonder what it was. It was certainly some sort of magic doorway! He decided that he would return with a couple of his servants and more rope. Someone else could have the honour of being the first to explore further!

He did not tell his servants what they would be doing when they obediently followed him on foot to the cave entrance a few days later. The servants were very unhappy about entering the cave, but he reassured them that he had been in before and that there was nothing to fear. Once inside they hesitated at the top of the boulder pile, but he managed to get them through it. While he was waiting for the last one to come through, he noticed that there was no draught as there had been on his first visit. He led them along the passage with their three torches flaming merrily and illuminating their way. When he reached the place where he had seen the black curtain, he had a surprise. They had arrived at a dead end! The passage ended in a flat wall of rock that filled the cave from floor to ceiling. The black curtain had vanished! He felt the rock-face with his hands, but it was completely solid and impenetrable. Had he been dreaming the last time that he was here? He searched high and low, but there was no sign of the black curtain. There was nothing to do except return to the entrance. The servants were very glad to do that before the goblins came to get them!

When he told his brother and sisters about his experience, they would not believe him and praised his story-telling ability. However, one of his brothers agreed to accompany him into the cave to see if he was telling the truth. The outcome was the same. There was a blank wall at the end of the cave and no black curtain. His brother told him that his vivid imagination had tricked him in the darkness, or else he had dreamt it. They returned home and never visited the cave again.

Over the years that followed, the local peasants claimed to have seen goblins, strange people and giants that gave credence to the legends of the forest, but they were never believed. As the society changed and people were better educated, the stories were treated as legends, even when some people out in the forest near the cave reported that they had seen 'small men' scurrying through the trees to hide from them. It was not until a couple of speleologists were exploring the caves in the area that anyone chose to tell them the legend, but they treated it as an attempt to keep them out of the cave. When they explored the cave, they were surprised that the passage was so straight and that it did not follow the limestone joints and beds of the local massif. They also were surprised that it ended in a blank wall. This presented them with a mystery. They reasoned that, from the line of the passage and from their knowledge of the local limestone, that there was no geological fault at that point which could have caused the sudden termination. The idea that it could have been an ancient mine was rejected, due to the absence of pick marks or signs of ore. They reported the puzzle to other speleologists, but none could come up with an answer and attempts to find one were quickly abandoned when a major cave system was discovered in the region. One day, however, some caver with curiosity will read the written records left by the speleologists and go to explore the cave again. Then, with luck, that wall may no longer be a blank one!

Adit

13
Alderley Edge Copper Mines

The Alderley Edge Copper Mines are on National Trust property near the delightful village of Alderley Edge in Cheshire. The area has been mined ever since the Bronze Age, about four thousand years ago. The mines were worked in Roman times, but the most significant production was in the nineteenth century. At one point, when copper mining was declining elsewhere in the British Isles, the mines were unusually productive, but, now, all have been closed for many years. As they were easily accessible from the large cities that lie around the Peak District, there have always been lots of visitors, not necessarily with any caving or mining experience. West Mine, Wood Mine and Engine Vein were once the playground of 'Teddy boys' and drop-outs, who left rubbish and caused significant damage in the mines. The mines are now gated, but bona-fide cavers and mining enthusiasts can obtain access and guides from the Derbyshire Caving Club.

Alderley Edge has a long history of copper mining, but it also has a history of magic, witchcraft and sorcery. Even today "The Edge" attracts pagans at 'Hallowe'en', Equinox and Solstice. There are many myths and legends about the mines. In particular, there is the legend of a wizard who needed a horse to complete the number of a sleeping army, hidden in caverns under "The Edge". It was predicted that there would come a day when this army would awake from its enchanted sleep and ride into battle to save the country. The wizard is remembered today in the name of the nearby restaurant and "The Wizard's Well".

"The Edge" always seems to have an air of mystery about it, whatever the season. The Cheshire author, Alan Garner, based his novel *"The Weirdstone of Brisingamen"* on the area and used his knowledge of the mines in writing it. (*In the novel the mines harboured malevolent creatures that were seeking the stone to bring about a new age of darkness*). His more recent novel *"Boneland"*, the third of his *"Weirdstone"* trilogy, is located around "Stormy Point", "Castle Rock", "Saddlebole" and "Beacon Lodge", all prominent landmarks on "The Edge" and ranges across time from prehistoric shamans to the present day technology of Jodrell Bank radio-telescope.

When I first moved to Cheshire, I was very interested in the mines as they were so near my home. The local cavers were very helpful and I made several visits into West Mine and Wood Mine with them. In the late 70's I occasionally used to lead groups into Wood Mine, but eventually, due to interests further afield, I did not go there again until in my seventies.

How ageing affects the memory adversely! When I went on a club visit to West Mine with an expert geologist and mineralogist, I had only vague memories of the complex of mine passages that I used to know so well. I was amazed at the number of metal ores that the mine contained. The main ores mined were malachite and azurite for extracting copper, but small amounts of lead and cobalt ores were also mined. Our guide was a real expert and, as well as showing us the main malachite deposits, he pointed out bright blue deposits of azurite and small vein deposits of ores containing cobalt, manganese, molybdenum, tungsten, nickel, vanadium and iron as we followed him around the mine. In various places there were small grey flecks of galena in the sandstone rocks, showing the presence of lead.

Apparently there were once very small quantities of gold there, too. The visit occupied several hours as West Mine is the largest of the Alderley Edge Mines. A visit to Wood Mine was proposed for later in the year.

Our visit to Wood Mine was arranged for a Tuesday evening in November. It was pitch dark, very cold and pelting with rain when we arrived at the meeting point. Howard Taylor, our guide, was the last to arrive, so we changed into our caving gear and cowered in the bushes, or in the back of a van, until he arrived. The footpath through Windmill Wood was very water-logged from the wettest summer on record and a week of heavy rain prior to our visit. At one point, we left the path and had to squelch through boggy ground that came half way up our wellies! When we eventually reached the mine entrance, I did not recognise it. It had been upgraded in the years of my absence and there was a new, well-constructed concrete plinth, with a small metal man-hole cover painted in bright yellow. Howard reached through the fist-sized hole in the cover to unlock the padlock underneath. He opened the lid and we lined up to descend the two steel ladders beneath it and escape from the cold and the drizzle. We alighted in a dry passage that was an old adit hewn out by the nineteenth century miners. The short, dry, passage led to a tee-junction and an open space containing various old mining implements. Here, we stopped to remove our waterproofs that had protected us from the elements on the surface. I felt pleased that I recognised this part of the mine from my previous visits many years ago.

Wood Mine has three basic levels, connected by fixed steel ladders, or climbs, and has about three miles of passages. However, although I remembered all of the key route markers, I had forgotten how they were connected to one another! We walked in single file along the passage and across a bridge over another passage in the level below until we came to 'Sand Cavern'. Here, we re-grouped, after one or two of our team had explored a side passage up a climb that came to a dead end. I was too busy talking to remember the route exactly after that, until we came to the descent at 'Chain Steps'. I remembered this obstacle clearly, but my creaky knees made the descent a slower one than the last time. We then continued into the 'Rabbit Caverns' and the 'Lower Hauling Level'. We diverted to see 'The Blue Lake', then the 'Hough Level' and followed the 'Railway Level' to 'Key Chamber'. Then we made our way to 'Junction Shaft' and climbed up its eight metre steel ladder back to 'Sand Cavern' again. I cannot remember what we did after that, except I have a vague idea that we passed through 'Stump Chamber' with its flat ceiling and a timber pit prop stuck in the middle. After that I remember sitting in a large chamber with a short crawl that left the chamber we were in and curved round to end in rather tight squeeze back into the chamber. Only a few of the fit and agile cavers did this. Howard and I sat in comfort watching them emerge hot and puffing from their exertions. Then we made our way to 'North End Chamber', the largest in the mine. We went up and down levels and at one point came to 'Birthday Chamber', where we went up a level again. There was some crawling and more walking until we finally arrived back at the junction near the entrance. Here, we took the left-hand passage and descended to admire 'The Green Waterfall' and more blue-green formations a bit further on. The beautiful blue-green coloration here was due to *Chrysocolla*, a hydrous copper silicate, coming out of solution from the trickling water. After the photographers had finished, we then returned to our starting point to put on our outdoor gear and prepare for the surface.

The whole trip was a dry one, with plenty of interesting things to see and with no insurmountable obstacles, or difficulties, to overcome. Apart from discovering that my memory was not as good as I had thought, I really enjoyed my outing, as did my companions. On the surface, the rain had stopped, but it was very cold as we walked back to our vehicles. We changed into our everyday clothing quickly and there was just enough time to go for a beer before closing time. I was glad to have had the privilege to enjoy such a pleasant and companionable caving trip so near to home. It was yet another experience to be stored for reminiscing in the future.

A year later, I re-visited Wood Mine with Bill Hester and we had a very enjoyable tour of the mine for me to refresh my knowledge of it. Bill was an enthusiastic and knowledgeable companion and agreed to arrange a trip later that year for Keith, Mike and Jenny who had never visited the mine. This was arranged in due course by e-mail and telephone.

The weather for our visit was the complete antithesis of my earlier November visit. It was high summer and roastingly hot! We were glad to get into the cool atmosphere of the mine. Bill insisted that I should lead us and acted as our historical and geological mentor as we toured the mine. I now knew the route and took the bridge from the adit entrance junction through 'Sand Cavern', down 'Chain Steps' to 'Rabbit Caverns', for a visit to 'The Blue Lake' and 'Hough Level' then through to 'Canal Turn', 'Stump Chamber' and through the sandy crawl to the 'North End Chambers'. We returned via the 'Green

Waterfall' and 'Seed Beds' to the ladder up to 'Sand Cavern' and then out. It's amazing how quickly one's memory can be revived! The main thing to do is to make sure that it is maintained regularly or lose it!

We all enjoyed this visit enormously, confirming that Wood Mine is ideally suited to the older caver. In addition, Keith, Mike and Jenny had their appetites whetted both for the mine and for the area. They asked for a return visit in the near future to explore West Mine and to spend some time walking 'On The Edge'.

Although largely the province of cavers and mining enthusiasts, non-caving groups, whose members are reasonably fit, are sometimes led on conducted tours in the mines. The Derbyshire Caving Club also organise open weekends for the public, with access to their museum and certain mines, too. Wood Mine provides an interesting and enjoyable expedition for anyone interested in mining history and is an ideal outing for older cavers and non-cavers who are fit and healthy.

14
Old Rope

Old rope is always a problem for cavers and mountaineers as it is difficult to decide whether to bin it, or to carry on using it. If it shows signs of wear, or abrasion, it may be rejected, especially if it has been in use for more than three years. If there is any doubt, it is possible to drop-test a sample, but cavers use their common sense and, if in doubt, they bin it. To a certain extent, it all depends on what is considered to be 'old'.

A similar problem applies to cavers themselves. When is a caver 'old'? Is it just a matter of years, or is it determined by the caver's physical and mental condition? Many cavers are not as old as their years suggest. The difference is difficult to tell without a test of some kind. Medical tests are helpful, but the best test is to enjoy and survive a hard caving trip. Apart from that, some people seem to be 'old' before their time. Youth is determined in the mind and not by the years. A caver is too old when he, or she, considers himself, or herself, to be unfit to go caving and hangs up their caving gear for good. Most cavers do this in their fifties, or sixties, but a considerable number continue well past the retirement age. These are the 'Older Cavers'! The 'Coffin Dodgers' who perform conservation, maintenance and odd jobs in the caves and mines of the Peak District, are all over sixty five years old, for example.

In the early days of caving, when ropes were hawser laid and made of natural materials such as hemp, manila, or sisal, the ropes used in caves had a relatively short life and even those in use were often not to be trusted. In those days, old rope rotted quickly if it was not kept dry. The early cavers constructed their ladders using hawser laid hemp ropes and these had the same problems. My first ever ladder descent was down Lancaster Hole. The first section was laddered with rope ladder with large wooden rungs that were easy to descend. Unfortunately, a few feet down, this ended and the rest of the pitch was rigged with the new 'Electron' ladder. This was constructed with steel cables and alloy rungs that were smaller and more difficult to descend. Luckily, I was life-lined down the hole on one of the 'new' hawser laid nylon ropes!

Old ropes remind me of my grandfather's barn. When I was a boy, I often spent holidays with my grandparents at Bury Green, in Hertfordshire. My grandfather was a thatcher. He ran a successful local business with my Uncle Arthur, thatching hay-ricks, barns and houses. They had a horse and cart, wooden ladders and lots of old hemp and manila ropes, used for their work. My grandfather never wasted anything and his barn was full of old rope, broken ladders, string, wooden stakes, dusty corn-sacks that they wore on wet days, all sorts of rusty iron implements, straw, hay and countless other items saved for potential use later. The barn had a particular musty smell about it that I can still remember. Perhaps some of this was due to the rotting of the old hemp rope!

The discovery of nylon revolutionised textile and rope manufacture. Nylon ropes were stronger, lighter, more elastic and water-resistant than hemp ropes. The original nylon process involved a complex chain of chemical reactions to produce Hexa-methylene-diamine and Adipic acid that were then reacted to form 'Nylon Salt' and polymerised to form Nylon 6,6. Other routes have been developed since then, such as that using Caprolactam to produce Nylon 6 and other nylons with longer polymer chains. *(The six refers to the number of carbon atoms in the repeating unit of the polymer chain)*. Most of the popular modern caving ropes are made from Nylon 6. Once the polymer has been made, it is melt extruded and pumped to spinnerets to form long filaments. Cold drawing these, to extend the length four times, or more, aligns the polymer chains and gives the tensile strength needed for rope-making.

Nylon ropes were originally used by mountaineers as protection against falls from height. The elasticity of these ropes gave a greater measure of protection to a falling climber than earlier, less elastic ropes. Cavers used this property for life-lining ladder climbers, but when single rope techniques (SRT) were developed, less elastic ropes were needed. Bouncing up and down on the end of an elastic rope at the bottom of a hundred metre shaft can be most unpleasant and even dangerous!

Other polymers are also used for making ropes, such as Polyethylene-terephthalate, Polypropylene and Polyethylene. The early use of polymeric ropes for SRT quickly revealed the danger of rope abrasion on underground pitches. There were several accidents when polypropylene ropes were not protected from abrasion, for example. Nowadays, caving ropes are usually of nylon with a 'kernmantel' construction. This construction has an outer, abrasion-resistant, sheath with a load-bearing inner core of polymer fibres. Less elastic, or 'Static' ropes, are made with the core untwisted and of polymer with longer polymer chains. Longer polymer chains are made chemically, or by treating nylon granules with shorter chains in the solid phase. Modern ropes are also water resistant and, if stored and handled carefully, can be safely used for a long time. An 'old rope' nowadays is usually more than three years old, but caving clubs always keep careful records of their communally used ropes and test them at the end of their life to decide when to take them out of service.

This a good point at which to take an interesting detour along a side passage into the caverns of the polythene world. In the late 60's I worked on the commissioning of the first computer-controlled high-pressure polythene plant in the world. I thus became a member of the community of chemists and engineers who worked on the ICI high pressure polythene process. In many ways we were similar to cavers, exploring new regions and taking calculated risks as we did so. High pressure polythene was discovered by accident in a high pressure laboratory in 1933 and an industrial process for its manufacture was developed to run for the first time in 1939, by ICI. Polythene was particularly valued for its low dielectric constant that made it an essential material for high frequency radio equipment. During the Second World War, the ICI process was kept secret as polythene coaxial cable was a key component of radar equipment. After the war, the ICI process was licensed to several industrial manufacturers and new catalysts were developed to ease manufacture. Once industrial scale processes were able to produce polythene in bulk, it was used for a plethora of useful plastic products ranging from mouldings such as table-ware, toys and toilet seats, to packaging films and fibres.

The high pressure process was highly exothermic and operated at pressures of several thousand times atmospheric. For example, we tested the reactors on the new plant to a pressure of 1650 atmospheres. The exothermic reaction and high pressures required a high level of engineering knowledge and skill to contain them, so the process was expensive, but profitable, in the early years. However, the development of the Zeigler and Natta catalysts in the 50's enabled processes that could be run at atmospheric pressures to produce 'High Density' polythene (HDPE) less expensively. HDPE was not as suitable for cable as the low density polythene (LDPE), so the high pressure process was diminished but not abandoned. Nowadays, there are many types of polythene, categorised by their density, molecular weight and structure. The commonest of these are LDPE, HDPE and LLDPE.

There have been significant developments in very high density and very high molecular weight polythenes that are suitable for ropes. Ultra-high-molecular weight polythene (UHMWPE) is used for ropes to moor ocean-going liners and oil-tankers, for example. The use of UHMWPE in caving ropes is in its infancy as ropes made from it would not be elastic enough. Including a few filaments of UHMWPE in the core of caving ropes may solve this problem in the future. We are now considering 'new' ropes and not 'old' ropes, so, at this point we need to return to the main passage again!

Old ropes contain their history well. It is difficult to see the effects of water, or mud, on the core, or the effects of sunlight on the sheath. Careful washing after a muddy trip and storage in a dry dark tackle store are essential if ropes are to survive to old age. The same applies to cavers. Past seventy, it is difficult to see the internal effects of the last seventy summers and winters of fun. The caver who has lived a healthy life does not often present many visible signs of age except for the loss of hair and skin texture and may very well be not as old as his, or her, years suggest. The acid test of an older caver is whether he, or she, can still enjoy caving. Taking a fall or drop test could be fatal, however!

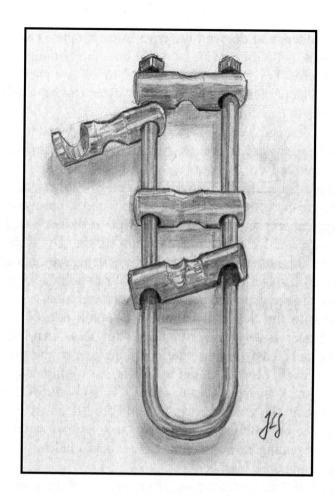

15
Sell Gill

Sell Gill pothole, near the Yorkshire village of Horton-in-Ribblesdale, was first explored by The Yorkshire Ramblers Club in 1897. It is about 80 metres deep and almost a quarter of a mile long, with a large chamber at the bottom. There are two entrances to the system, the 'Normal' or 'Dry Route' and the 'Wet Route'. The 'Wet Route' follows the surface stream down 'Goblin Shaft', a 46 metres deep pitch that can only be descended safely in dry weather. The 'Dry Route' is often used to train beginners and it was there that I led my first ladder trip in the early 60's. As a consequence, I always have a slight sense of nostalgia when I go down this route. Nowadays, cavers rarely use ladders and descend the cave using Single Rope Technique (SRT). In fact, Sell Gill provides a really good opportunity for training in SRT as the 'Dry Route' is passable in all weathers, if rigged correctly. It is a particularly good cave for older cavers to enjoy and to practise their SRT skills, too.

I usually descend Sell Gill by the 'Dry Route' once a year in an attempt to keep myself fit and to practise my Single Rope Technique. The last time that I did this was with Keith, just before he reached the youthful age of seventy. We drove to Horton-in-Ribblesdale, parked in the paying car-park that conveniently has good toilets, changed into our caving gear and set off for the cave without further ado. I carried a 100metre rope and Keith a 20metre rope to rig the 'Dry Route'. As we crossed over the hump-back bridge in the village, we noticed that the beck was in full spate. However, there had been no rain for a couple of days, so we did not expect to get very wet underground.

The walk to the Sell Gill entrances is uphill and over a mile in length. The track is very stony in places, with occasional large puddles that do not make easy going underfoot. This part of the trip, with the rope on my back, always seems to be the least enjoyable part! Half way up the track there is a gate where I usually stop for a breather before continuing to the entrance, but this time I felt fitter than usual and we carried on without stopping. By the time that we arrived, both of us were sweating in our caving clothes and glad to put down our tackle bags and take a breather.

The two Sell Gill entrances are on either side of the track. The 'Wet Route' is to the right when approaching from Horton, and the 'Dry Route' to the left, down a gulley. The Wet route was taking a fast flowing stream that looked as if it was still in flood and the pothole was emitting a loud roaring sound from the falling water below. We scrambled down the gulley to a rocky shelf where we stopped to put on our SRT gear. For those who are not familiar with SRT, some explanation is worthwhile:

We each wore a 'sit-harness' that consisted of a waist belt with thigh loops stitched to it and the two ends held together by a *'D-shaped Maillon Rapide'* steel link instead of a buckle. The *'D-shaped Maillon'* provided the main anchor point for our weight and all of the rest of our rope climbing equipment. We each had an ascender linked to a chest harness, a descender, cow's-tails, and the hand-jammer security cord attached to the 'D'. We also used the 'D' to clip in a spare cow's-tail attached to tackle bags for holding the rope. The waist harness also had a couple of loops for attaching extra items, such as a spare ascender, spare carabiners, or small equipment bags. The hand-jammer with its foot-loops attached for ascending, could also be clipped into a carabiner in a waist loop to keep it out of the way when descending. Once equipped with all of this tackle, in spite of our tatty oversuits, we looked like modern cavers should!

The 'Dry Route' was well equipped with the latest steel 'Eco' anchors, so we only needed carabiners to attach the ropes to them on all of the pitches. In the past, we used to have to drill out holes with self-tapping bolts in the rock-face and attach hangers, but this practise has been superceded on popular routes to avoid peppering the rock with holes. Needless to say, the modern 'Eco hangers' make life simpler and safer, provided that they are properly installed. Nevertheless, many 'old' cavers resent them on the basis that they encourage young cavers to follow rigidly marked routes and become competitive 'rope gymnasts'.

This presents an interesting case in point regarding the symptoms of 'old age' compared with the symptoms of not feeling so old after seventy. Change is inevitable in this world and cannot be avoided whether it is for good or evil. Although not all changes are beneficial, those that are should be adopted as quickly and effectively as possible in the opinion of an older caver. Lots of 'old' cavers were very much against SRT when it first came in and some even named it 'Silly Rope Tricks' as a sign of their derision. Needless to say, they were left behind. In my particular case, it opened up the big pitches overseas that I would have found too tiring on ladder. SRT also made caving a modern, light-weight and professional sport with a higher level of exploration and safety than previously. The same applies to many beneficial changes that seem abhorrent to 'old' people, such as the development of the Internet. It seems such a shame that many 'old' people, isolated in their homes because they never took an interest in computers, could have friends and family to see and talk to on SKYPE at the touch of a 'mouse'! We should never stop learning. Life is full of interesting and educative opportunities. Education is a wonderful process that has advanced humanity through the centuries by enabling change to be implemented effectively in all aspects of life.

Abandoning my wandering thoughts for the reality of the cave, I climbed further down the gulley to rig the first pitch. I then descended the gulley, running the rope through my rack and squeezed through the narrows that led to the top of the first pitch. Here, I locked off my rack and clipped my long cow's-tail in to one of the anchors in the rock face above the next section of the pitch. Below me, I could see the floor of the cave, with its jumble of rocky bits and pieces glistening wetly green in the daylight. Facing me was the grey limestone wall of the pothole, with its small cracks and slimy foot-holes. There were several 'Eco' hangers sunk into this wall for rigging the pitch. I tied a 'Y' knot in the slack of the 20 metre rope, attached it to two of these anchors and adjusted the lengths of the 'Y' to share the load equally between the two anchors. I then clipped my short cow's-tail into one of the carabiners, unlocked my rack and descended until the short cow's-tail took my full weight. I was then able to take the rack out of the top rope section and thread it into the bottom section of rope hanging from the 'Y-hang' and lock it off again. There was small ledge for my feet so that I could then lift myself up, release the short cow's-tail and lower myself on to the rack. Satisfied that it was secure, I released the long cow's-tail, unlocked the rack and descended the pitch. This particular set of manoeuvres is a regular routine for a descent past a rope anchor when using SRT, but is described here for the benefit of those who are not familiar with it. In the old days, we would have attached an 'Electron' ladder to a suitable rock using a wire tether and just lobbed it down the pitch for a descent with a safety rope! Maybe the 'old' folk led a simpler, if tackle-heavy and muscle-bound, life!

The pitch was quite slippery and dripping with water after the recent rains, so, near the bottom, I kicked against the rock to swing out and land on the floor of the cave away from the drips. The rocky floor had all sorts of storm debris from above, together with bits and pieces of rubbish left by careless cavers. I quickly unclipped my rack and shouted up to Keith that the rope was free. While Keith was descending, I turned my lamp on and went down into the cave, over the dry, white, boulders that were out of daylight, carrying the big rope in its tackle bag. There was a short easy climb down to a landing at the top of the next pitch, where I waited for Keith to arrive. I noticed that there was a shower of water drops sparkling in the black void ahead. There was also a steady rain falling from the roof, but I knew that we could rig the pitch away from of this to keep ourselves dry.

The second pitch is over ten metres deep, with a small ramp of a ledge on the left-hand wall that enables a caver to traverse away from the water shower. There was a plethora of 'Eco' anchors, like chicken-pox, on both walls and along the ramp, so I had plenty of choice! I tied the end of the big rope to an anchor in the left-hand wall and handed the tackle bag to Keith. He clipped himself in to another anchor and pulled out enough rope to rig a traverse line out to the end of the ledge. Here, he fixed a 'Y-Belay' to two anchors that were set in the wall, to hold the rope for the pitch. Satisfied with the belay, he threaded the rope into his descender and went a short way down the rope. He then straddled across the pitch on small footholds to attach a loop of tape to an anchor in the opposite wall. He was then able to deflect the rope away from the wall by a 'deflection belay', made by passing the rope that he had descended through a carabiner clipped in to the tape loop. Then, as he descended further, the 'deflection belay' held the rope away from the wall to prevent it from rubbing on the rock-face further down. He then continued down into the large chamber below, with the rope running freely out of the tackle bag hanging from his waist harness.

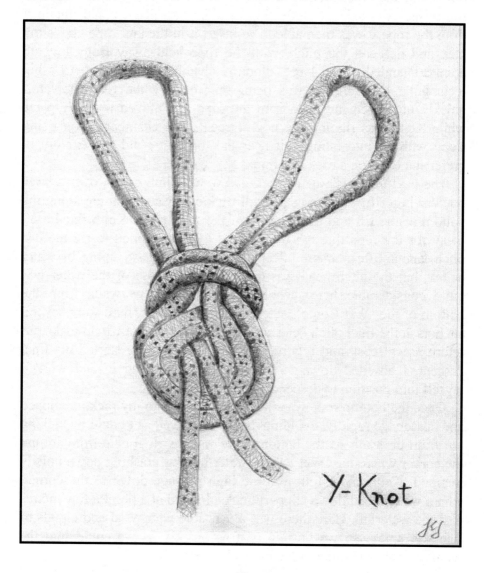

Y-Knot

On my first descent here, I secured a ladder to a tether at the top and threw it down the pitch to hang straight through the showering water, regardless. A safety rope was then used to protect each caver descending, held securely by a caver at the top. In those days life was simpler, but wetter! This time, I went across the traverse, with my cow's-tails clipped in to the traverse line for protection and waited at the end until Keith shouted that the rope was free. The rope in the tackle bag was enough for the rest of the descents, so he carried on down to fix it in place while I was descending.

Once the rope was free, I threaded it through my rack, unclipped my protection and descended as far as the 'deflection belay'. Here, I pulled some slack through the deflecting carabiner so that I could unclip it from the rope. I was then able to re-insert it in the taut rope above my rack and descend the pitch, with the rope held away from any rub points. I landed in the large, gloomy, chamber below, next to a big rectangular boulder that was being splashed by the roof shower. I quickly unclipped my rack from the rope and moved to a dry place while Keith was rigging the next descent. The chamber had a rising slope with an interesting exit near the top, but I did not explore it, preferring to sit on a rock and think!

The next obstacle was a short, awkward, climb down, over a large boulder in a rift. There was a small trickle of water running along the bottom of the rift and over the lip of the final pitch. Keith fixed a Y-belay for the rope through the rift and then descended to rig the last pitch, about fifteen metres deep. There was a heavy spray of water below, but the pitch head was quite dry. The noise of the water was quite considerable here, echoing around the cave walls from the bottom of the 'Wet Route' waterfall further down. There were several anchors at the final pitch head and Keith used two that would make our return ascent easy and relatively dry. As soon as he started his final descent, I abseiled down to the pitch head, clipped in and worked myself into position to descend.

Once the bottom rope was free I threaded it into my rack, unclipped and descended rapidly, avoiding the spray as well as I could by kicking out from the wall. At the bottom there was a virtual gale from around the corner where the 'Wet Route' waterfall was crashing down noisily in flood. Keith and I followed the high passage down to the corner, where we climbed down slippery rocks, to land at a point a few metres past the waterfall. Here there was a veritable whirlwind and clouds of fine wet spray, so we hurried past as quickly as we could into the relative peace and quiet of the main chamber.

The main chamber of Sell Gill is quite impressive, but it does not have the imposing grandeur of a major cave and always has a friendly atmosphere about it. There are several routes down to the bottom, all over boulders, some of which are slippery with mud and calcite. We made our separate ways down to where the stream was running merrily over the rocks and pebbles in its bed. Then we paddled in the water, around a bend in the passage, into a well decorated part of the cave with white, glittering, stalactites and stalagmites on the walls and in grottoes high above the stream. Here, the stream ran over boulders and pebbles that had been stained and blackened by the peaty water from the surface. The contrast between the blackened pebbles and the brilliant whiteness of the formations was really striking.

I paused to admire my surroundings before continuing down-stream. In a short distance, we came to a low section of passage that ended in a wet, bible-black, crawl. Since neither of us wanted a wetting, we decided to turn back here and retraced our steps up to the top of the chamber. I chose a climb that led around to the left when ascending and I suddenly realised that it went quite a way off route when I saw Keith's light on the other side of the chamber. I quickly rejoined Keith and we scrambled back up, past the roaring waterfall and the whirlwind of spray, to reach the bottom of our rope.

Normally, we take turns to rig and de-rig, but Keith kindly allowed me to go up first. I pulled my chest harness tight and released the cam on my chest ascender so that I could insert the rope and then closed it. The cam bit into the rope, so that it could only move upwards and it supported any downwards pull on the ascender. I opened the cam on my hand-jammer and inserted it into the rope above shoulder height and closed it to provide the same function. Holding the loose end of the rope in my hand, I lifted myself up to raise the chest ascender and then used my weight to take up the slack in the rope, pushing the hand-jammer up until I was fully supported by the rope. I put my feet into the foot-loop hanging from the hand-jammer and stood up, moving my chest ascender up as I did so. It was then a matter of pushing the hand-jammer up, lifting myself up in the foot-loop to raise the chest ascender and then letting it take my weight for another push up of the hand-jammer. By repeating this sequence of movements, I made an easy ascent to the top of the pitch. Here, I clipped my long cow's-tail into one of the rope anchors before transferring my ascenders on to the rope above the belay. I found it was quite straightforward to cross the anchors at the top of the pitch due to Keith's careful rigging. I shouted that the rope was free and climbed up the next section, still using my ascenders as the climb was rather awkward for my arthritic knees.

I then waited for Keith in the chamber below the second pitch whilst he de-rigged on his way up. As soon as he arrived, he asked me to carry on up the next pitch to save time as I am usually the slowest climber. Again, I made an easy ascent, the first part free-hanging and the last section against the rock. By the time that I had passed the deflection belay and landed on the ledge at the top, Keith was ready to ascend. I traversed off the pitch and Keith soon arrived to finish de-rigging the pitch and the traverse line. I helped to pull up the tackle bag of rope and stuffed the rest of the rope into the tackle bag to finish off the job. We then returned to daylight and made our exit up the top pitch back to the surface, de-tackling as we went.

On the surface, the sun shone brightly. We were both hot and sweaty, but refreshed by the open air and a chilly breeze blowing across the gulley. Our trip had not taken us very long, but had been most enjoyable, satisfying and invigorating. It felt really great to be alive! We soon divested ourselves of our SRT gear and, with the rope and tackle bags on our backs, strode off downhill along the track back to Horton and lunch. As we walked in the sunshine, we enjoyed the beautiful views around us, happily sorting out the world's problems on the way. We older cavers can certainly enjoy ourselves, even if no-one listens to us!

16
Old Bangers

Cavers over seventy years of age are like old bangers! Although they keep going, they need constant maintenance and repair. Luckily, restoration and spare parts are available, thanks to the National Health Service, but regular, effective, maintenance over the years can make these unnecessary in some cases. Several old bangers have had rebores (*Angioplasty*) or have had turbo-chargers fitted (*Bypass surgery*). Most have had their water and exhaust systems de-coked earlier in their lives. One of the main problems with old bangers, however, is rust in the suspension system (*Arthritis*). The same problem applies to the transmission, particularly the joints. For some old bangers the suspension has had to be replaced (*Prosthetic surgery*). Some avoid this expensive solution as long as possible by using advanced lubrication (*Anti-inflammatories*), while the others just creak and groan. Back seat operations are usually still possible thanks to Viagra, but long journeys, bumpy surfaces, narrow lanes and steep hills require patience.

Although old bangers usually have dents and scratches on their bodywork, some have looks that are quite respectable and belie their age. With a good set of tyres and regular maintenance, they are completely road-worthy. The most important components, however, are hidden from view, or under the bonnet! The brakes must work effectively to avoid destruction in a crash and must pass the annual testing, so these are rarely a problem unless they stick on. The gear-box may make a noise, but can, nevertheless, enable an old banger to accelerate and put in a reasonable performance uphill. The windows, hand-brake, heating, windscreen wipers and head lights are all manual. An old banger is normally very practical and uncomplicated. However, the older the banger, the dimmer the headlights and, unfortunately, the horn does not usually work as well as it used to. The key component, however, is the driver. Most old bangers have young drivers because these cannot afford new cars. The trouble with such drivers is that they take more risks than older drivers and the old bangers tend to wear out more quickly as a result. On the other hand, anyone who has followed an old banger with an old driver will find them wearisome. An old banger can be good fun with a young driver! It is an important fact that it is generally the younger drivers who keep the old bangers on the road.

If a young caver sees an old banger groaning and creaking uphill, it is of no use hooting. The best solution is to try and relieve the banger's load by taking on some luggage or giving a tow up the hill. Once over the top, old bangers roll downhill easily!

17
Maintenance

Anyone who is in their seventies, or older, requires good maintenance to enjoy life to the full. Although the author is not fully qualified to advise anyone on this subject, it is so important that it may be worthwhile to share a few observations, ideas and opinions about it.

The aim here is to enjoy life as much as possible, so severe regimens and hypochondria are excluded. Nevertheless, one should always be on guard against sudden changes in one's health in order to take evasive action. Apart from the physical symptoms due to a variety of cancers and other bodily malfunctions, there are all sorts of nasty micro-organisms around and it is difficult to avoid an occasional attack by one of them. A key way of protecting yourself from these is to try and keep clear of crowded, humid, aerosol-clouded areas, such as those in aeroplanes, supermarkets and pubs. However, if you are a gregarious person, this is not an option! In the winter, it may be practical to wear gloves around the shops and pubs and to wash one's hands with one of those alcoholic preparations that are reputed to kill germs before touching the eyes, mouth, or before eating. Although there are antibiotics available to treat most human pathogens nowadays, they do not attack viruses.

Flu is caused by a virus and can hit suddenly and severely. Antibiotics will not treat it. People over the age of sixty five are at risk of getting flu more severely and are more at risk of experiencing complications such as bronchitis, or pneumonia. It is thus a good idea for older folk to have a flu vaccination.

If you catch a virus and the symptoms last for more than a couple of days, it is a good idea to consult your general practitioner (GP) for advice. Unfortunately, as most viruses cannot be cured by medicines, unless there is a vaccination available, the sufferer's auto-immune system needs time to overcome them. Resting, drinking plenty of fluids and taking over-the-counter painkillers will help in the acute stage. Anyway, this paragraph has digressed away from maintenance, so let us return to it:

A human being is a very complex biological system that requires careful maintenance and repair. For many years, this system has been considered as a mixture of 'Mind, Body and Spirit', with the whole greater than the sum of its parts. The concept of 'Holistic' medicine, as opposed to 'Specialist' medicine, has been developed along the same lines. It thus seems a good idea to maintain ourselves holistically.

It is widely accepted that a healthy life-style should include plenty of exercise, a healthy diet, lots of demanding mental activity, a good night's sleep, enthusiasm for a pastime or project, a sustainable set of beliefs and companionship. It goes without saying that caving can provide most of these assets! Nevertheless, anyone can choose a maintenance routine to suit themselves without taking up caving. The key activity is, however, to keep up the routine.

There is lots of evidence that regular aerobic exercise is good for the health. The exercise does not have to be violent! The idea of "No gain without pain!" is not a good one, especially for older people, but it is a good idea to get sweaty. Walking over hilly ground for half an hour or more a day is reputed to be most beneficial, for example. Swimming for the same period is also very good, especially for those with arthritic joints. Some people find that exercise systems such as Yoga and Pilates are beneficial, but, again, many older people would not be supple enough to take these up, unless they had practised them when younger. There are other exercises such as Tai Chi that may be an answer to this problem, however. Most men and women will have pulled a muscle in their lives, or will have had back trouble that made them consult a physiotherapist. It is a good idea that the exercises prescribed to ease and correct these complaints should be continued regularly thereafter to avoid a repetition of the problem.

Raised blood pressure (hypertension) is a silent problem that increases the risks of strokes and heart attacks. It can be easily and painlessly checked with a home monitor, or at your local doctor's. Ideally, your blood pressure reading should be below 120/80mmHg, but anything under 130/80 is generally considered to be normal.

The subject of diet and nutrition is a difficult one as there are so many different and changing expert opinions about what is best. The idea of eating lots of fruit and vegetables, "Five a Day", together with plenty of lean protein and oily fish seems very sensible, as is the avoidance of saturated fats, too much salt, sugar and alcohol. Personally, the idea that red wine and dark chocolate are good for you seems very appealing, however! One aspect that has to be watched is body weight. Obesity can be a killer. It is a good idea to consult a graph of Body Mass Index (BMI) against your weight to determine whether you need to lose weight or not. Depending on the result, you may have to diet and take more exercise. It is a good idea to weigh yourself once a week and keep a record so you can see any changes over the long term.

Older people often suffer a deficiency of certain vitamins and some take 'multi-vitamins' to overcome this, although a balanced diet and sensible lifestyle should make this unnecessary. It is a good idea to top up your vitamin D out in the sunshine, or by eating oily fish and eggs, for example. Although it is common knowledge that fish oils are good for the cardio-vascular system and joints, the author has been taking 1000mg Cod Liver Oil every day for decades, but still has arthritic knees! Many people believe that large doses of vitamin C are a protection against diseases and cancer, with any excess being safely excreted, but this effect seems uncertain. There are sometimes deficiencies in minerals such as Iron, Zinc, Selenium and Copper that the body uses in small quantities, requiring suitable supplements to be taken. The world of nutrition is a minefield for most of us and a significant source of income for the nutritionists and pharmacists, but beyond the scope of a full treatment in this book. However, if you are interested in a deeper knowledge of this subject you can do your own research using the power of the Internet, local library or educational centres.

The nightmare of Dementia, or Alzheimer's disease, in old age is a frightening one. As we are now living longer, it has become more common, too. There are several practical ideas and opinions about how to minimise the risks, however. The main one seems to be "Use it or lose it!" It is considered to be very important to keep one's mind active. For example, research indicates that bi-lingual people who develop dementia do so two to three years later than people who only speak one language. One wonders what happens to tri or multi-lingual people! Mental activity can be stimulated by thousands of other disciplines than language, however, so you only have to choose your favourite. Music, painting, sculpture, literature, theatre, poetry, ballet, cooking, gardening, science and technology are but a few of the avenues to explore and learn. Crosswords, Puzzles, Su Doku, Brain teasers and countless other amusements, computerised or not, are also beneficial on a daily basis. The Internet is full of wonderful opportunities for research and education to inspire you and to tax your brain cells.

The working of the human mind is not fully understood, but many learned papers and books have been written on the subject. One idea studied is that of the subconscious mind. A maintenance task that you may find important, therefore, is to tune the working of your subconscious. Our subconscious seems to obey its own rules and works away without our knowing. For example, you must have had the experience of being unable to solve a puzzle, or a crossword clue and abandoned the problem. Then, a few hours, or even days later, the solution suddenly occurs to you. Who knows how this happened? Perhaps your subconscious was working away at it all of the time? When faced with any problem it is a well-known idea to 'sleep on it', indicating that people have known about this phenomenon for ages. It seems that the subconscious, although outside our direct awareness and control, can be maintained to our advantage if we make the effort. So it is a good idea to fill it full of positive ideas and thoughts on a regular basis. You are probably being fed a plethora of negative thoughts by the media and you must try and keep these out! If you believe that you can do something subconsciously, it is surprising what you can achieve!

One problem that sometimes afflicts older people is loneliness, often after the death of a partner or close friend. Loneliness sometimes causes depression. There are pharmaceutical products and Cognitive Behaviour Therapy (CBT) for treating serious depression, but, if the depression is temporary, it may be dispelled by plenty of exercise to raise the level of endorphins in the bloodstream and by an all-absorbing project of some kind, outside the constraints of the self. The subject is beyond the scope of this book as each of us is unique and our reactions to the problems of life are consequently all different.

Having briefly discussed the maintenance of Mind and Body, we need to consider how to maintain the spirit. The word 'Spirit' is a difficult word to interpret, especially as there are so many opinions as to what and where it is. Nevertheless, the word is useful for attempting to describe a human characteristic that is indescribable! Words are never reality and, in the same way that maps are not the ground, often lead to mis-interpretation. Spirit is a good example of this. We often speak of children as being 'High Spirited' and of an environment as being 'Dispiriting', so it is possible from common usage to gather some idea of what it means to the population at large. In the human context, it may have something to do with the idea of a person's very being or 'Self'. One thing is very clear, it is easier to perceive the spirit of someone else than to recognise your own! Either way, it is an important function to maintain, but you will have to find out how to do it yourself! One idea that may help, is to feed the question into your subconscious by meditating on the topic. Alternatively, you could do more research, seek expert advice, or attend a course on the subject. Hopefully, this chapter has stimulated you to think deeply about your maintenance. If not, then re-read it, although it might be wiser to move on as the last few paragraphs are recursive!

18
Ogof Ffynnon Ddu

The saga of Ogof Ffynnon Ddu is worthy of a complete book, so the brief précis here will hardly do it justice. However, the key elements of the story need to be told for those unfamiliar with the long and exciting epic of its discovery and exploration.

Ogof Ffynnon Ddu (OFD) is located in the Swansea valley near the village of Abercrave. In the 1940's it was known that the water sinking high in the hills above the valley at Pwll Byfre resurged at Ffynnon Ddu down in the bottom of the valley. Although there were no known cave passages near these points at that time, it seemed certain that there must be a large cave system between the sink and resurgence. Digging and diving at sink and resurgence over many months did not resolve the puzzle. However, the patience and perseverance of the local cavers eventually paid off and the cave was first entered in 1946 by Peter Harvey and Ian Nixon after many weeks spent digging near the resurgence. The cave, called OFD, had a sump at one end and an active stream-way as far as a large chamber blocked by a boulder choke. 'Boulder Chamber' marked the end of about a quarter of a mile of stream-way that was only a small part of the distance between sink and resurgence. Dives in the OFD sump were unsuccessful and the cave was explored for many years, with attempts to by-pass the sump via a dry high level system. Additionally, there were other digs nearby and one in the Cwm Dwr quarry revealed a cave system with a stream that was traced to connect with OFD. Digging in the choke at 'Boulder Chamber' in the 1950's eventually revealed 'Hush Sump' that was dived for some distance without further progress.

In 1960 there was a revival of interest and more digging in the boulders at 'Boulder Chamber' by-passed 'Hush Sump', but ended at 'Dip Sump'. This was dived for a considerable distance to 'The Shrimp Series'. In 1966, a concerted effort by divers Charles George, John Osborne and Terry Moon eventually enabled them to break through into the magnificent stream-way of OFD2 and, shortly afterwards, the further reaches now known as OFD3. Inspired by this discovery, in 1967, cavers broke a way through from Cwm Dwr. Continuing exploration from the stream-way by climbing 'Maypole Inlet' revealed the extensive 'Upper Series'. It soon became evident that a surface connection might be possible from this series. Finally, a rudimentary radio-detection system directed a surface dig that opened the 'Top Entrance' into the system. In the following years, with the combined efforts of many cavers and cave divers, the system was extended considerably to make it the deepest cave in Britain, with over thirty miles of passages. The system is very beautiful, sporting, and extensive, with a long and exciting stream-way.

Since the original explorations, several changes to the access arrangements have taken place. The OFD2 'Top Entrance' and Cwm Dwr are now located on a National Nature Reserve that is administered by Natural Resources Wales (NRW). An NRW permit is required for any cavers visiting them, or coming out of them after a through trip from OFD1. NRW permits can be obtained annually by reputable caving clubs, or for specific visits, by contacting the Ogof Ffynnon Ddu Management Committee Permit Secretary beforehand. The details of access arrangements can be found on the South Wales Caving Club (SWCC) website www.swcc.org.uk

For many years OFD has been a veritable magnet for cavers from all over Britain and other parts of the world as it is so interesting, beautiful and challenging to explore. The traverse from the bottom of the system near its resurgence through Ogof Ffynnon Ddu (OFD1), to

85

emerge at the top entrance of Ogof Ffynnon Ddu (OFD2), or the reverse, from top to bottom, is particularly enjoyable and challenging. For all cavers there are many different routes to explore in the system that will suit all ages and abilities. A popular favourite for older cavers is the OFD1 'Round Trip' via the lower streamway, 'Low's Passage', 'The Rawl Series', 'Pi Chamber' and the wire traverses high above the stream-way back to the exit. The OFD2 'Upper Series' provides many choice routes for older cavers who are reasonably fit, too. 'The Columns', not far from 'Top Entrance', are very beautiful and photogenic, but only accessible on specific days of the year and are well worth visiting. 'The White Arch' series also has plenty of interesting grottoes and passages to interest older cavers. The round trip from 'Top Entrance', down 'Salubrious Passage' into 'Selenite Passage' and back via 'Cross Rift' is a firm favourite for many cavers. The descent to the stream-way via 'Salubrious Passage', 'The Maze' and 'Maypole Aven', or via 'The Nave' and 'Second Oxbow' gives access to 'Top Waterfall'. These are just a few of the many routes possible and newcomers can spend many hours exploring the full extent of this complex and beautiful system.

The OFD3 system is for the young, agile, cavers and most over-seventies might hesitate to cross the difficult traverses at the end of OFD2 that lead towards it. Nevertheless, the routes through to OFD3 from 'Top Entrance' have many side passages that are of interest. For example, a trip across 'Poached Egg Climb' gives access to the 'Nyth Bran' series and 'The Crevasse'. One can descend 'The Crevasse' on SRT, climb down into the stream-way via the pitches in 'Pendulum Passage' and return by climbing 'Maypole Inlet' and negotiating 'The Maze' that follows, back into 'Salubrious Passage' again to make a round trip. The possibilities are endless!

One of the problems with large complex cave systems that attract lots of visitors is how to avoid, or handle, underground incidents. There is also a problem, when several caving teams are in the system at the same time, of how to keep track of them all. Anyone who thinks that cavers are disorganised, should go and inspect the cave trip logging system in the SWCC HQ. As explained previously, the cave management system is based on gated access, with visits booked and specific permits issued by the OFD management committee on behalf of Natural Resources Wales (NRW). Keys to the entrances are formally issued to bonafide cavers and caving clubs on presentation of a NRW permit when they arrive in person at the SWCC HQ. The system of tracking the visits, used at the time of writing, is as follows:

The leader of a trip, having presented his, or her, permit, is given a numbered key to the entrance that will be used for the trip. He fills in a 'Trip ticket' with his, or her name, the cave key number, the details of the route to be taken, the names and affiliations of the cavers in the team, any relevant car numbers, the entry time and an expected exit time. The 'Trip tickets' are provided in a pad that makes a second copy: One ticket goes on the hook in the locked cupboard that the key came from; the other is hung on a board clearly visible in the HQ foyer with a hook for every hour of the day. Once the trip has been completed, the key is returned to the cupboard and the leader takes the ticket off the display board and posts it in a small box below. The tickets are then retained for the cave records. This system ensures that the board in the foyer shows when the group is expected out and can act as a warning if they are overdue.

Knowing that a safe and well-run system exists is a great comfort to those who go underground and to their families on the surface. With such good foundations, the next step is to have as enjoyable a caving trip as possible. For myself, I have had so many really enjoyable and sporting trips in OFD that it is difficult to pick an example. Nowadays, since I passed the age of seventy, the range has diminished somewhat, but I particularly remember one most enjoyable trip that I did into 'Top Entrance' with Iain Miller, Steve Pearson-Adams, Mick Potts and Heather Simpson in 2011. It was Steve and Mick's first trip into the system, so they were particularly impressed by the superb underground scenery and the sporting caving that they encountered. Their enthusiasm and obvious delight contributed to a memorable trip. As a bonus, we had the benefit of Iain's vast knowledge of the system, gained from his work with the team that was re-surveying the system at that time. Iain has helped to keep me caving for some time and has always been willing to go caving with me as his rather slow and arthritic companion, without complaint. He also provides a repertoire of entertaining routes and short-cuts that I never knew existed. Heather and I had been in this part of the system many times so, for us, this was a nostalgia trip with extra interest provided by Iain.

It had rained heavily during the week, so we chose a route that we thought would not be affected by too much water, yet would be sporting and enjoyable. Luckily it was not raining as we walked up the hill from the South Wales Caving Club premises, so we could wear light over-suits. Nevertheless, we arrived at the entrance warm and sweaty, but otherwise dry. I unlocked the gate, retaining the key in my tackle bag for safety and entered the cave. Here, I turned off my light and waited for the others to come in. I needed some time to allow my eyes to adjust to the darkness! My eyes took longer to accommodate than those of my younger companions, who were ready to go as soon as they were inside.

Iain entered last and slammed the gate shut. Once all the lights were working, I led off down the slope into a large well-decorated passage. We were soon at a passage on the left that led to the tersely named 'Big Chamber Near the Entrance'. Iain and I described this to Steve and Mike as we paused briefly nearby before continuing on our way. I decided that we could visit this large chamber, with its tiresome floor of big boulders, on the way out if anyone wanted to. After skirting a pit in the floor on sloping banks of hardened mud deposits, we came to a large open chamber, with a boulder-strewn floor and water dripping from the roof on to a patch of flowstone. There were several ways off here and Iain pointed out the way up to the 'White Arch' series for Steve and Mick's benefit. Our planned route was straight ahead. We scrambled over several large slippery boulders and, where the passage became rift-like and narrow, took a right turn into a dry passage that led across a narrow ridge of hardened mud on rock, to a large junction. To our left was a dried out pool with white deposits, useful as a route marker on our return. Here, we went straight across into a dry, well-worn, passage that eventually led to the beginning of 'Gnome Passage'. As we followed this route, I took more care than usual and occasionally stopped to point particular way-markers for Steve and Mick's benefit on the return. The general idea was that they would lead us back out so that they could learn the route for their future visits.

We paused on the boulders at the head of the high vault of 'Gnome Passage', using our head-lights on full beam for better illumination for Steve and Mick to admire the stumpy, little, white, stalagmites peeping out from among the rocks. They looked just like garden gnomes! After that, we turned left into 'Chasm Passage' and continued past the white 'Wedding Cake' formation until we came to a very large open area littered with large, slippery boulders. The route to 'The Chasm' was straight ahead, but our way was down to the left. We descended steeply over the boulders at first, then against the left-hand wall to the entry of 'The Corkscrew'. This was an interesting move beneath a large boulder. There was a deep drop to one side of a flat ledge on which we sat to slither into position and enter a short squeeze under the boulder. The route here was so well worn that the surfaces were quite slippery, making the manoeuvre well lubricated and easy. A steep, slippery, climb down in a rift followed, that finally ended in a junction with 'Salubrious Passage', echoing with the noise of a small stream.

There was a small ledge to the left of the climb. Instead of continuing down to the stream running across the passage floor, we carefully stepped on to this ledge and followed it around, so that we could traverse above the stream for some distance. This avoided getting our feet wet in the deep pools below. Heather was impressed with this manoeuvre as she normally went down to the water here. Finally, however, we had to drop into the water and paddle downstream over the rocks, until we came to a small waterfall, noisily jetting out into a rift below. Here, we straddled the rift on small ledges and traversed out to avoid the water again. We were then able to continue traversing above the stream for some considerable way downstream. Eventually, we had to re-enter the stream and paddle until we came to a section where the passage floor was covered in 'Moon-milk' deposits. The countless cavers' boots had worn these down considerably from their original pristine condition over the years. The surface was still creamy white and slippery, nevertheless. It provided a salubrious, soapy, lightness, to the passage until the floor became flatter and the stream ran shallow between boulders and pebbles.

We continued further on and turned left into a narrow, dry, passage that wound through to the chamber where the aptly named 'Trident', a large forked stalactite hanging from the ceiling, was to be seen. We paused for Steve to take photos, then paddled around the corner, past 'The Judge' in his flowstone wig, into a boulder-strewn passage that eventually led to a short climb down to a busy streamway that ran across it. Here, we took a passage on the left, aptly named 'Swamp Creek'. This was meant to be an interesting diversion for Heather, who had not visited it before. The 'Swamp Creek' stream was near its flood level, but delightfully clean and refreshing after our hot and sweaty caving so far. I led the way, through water, above my waist in places, stopping occasionally to admire the beautiful white formations in the roof and along the walls. The grottoes and formations here have never been touched and are brilliantly white and striking to see. Iain, with better knowledge than me, traversed above the water and kept himself dry! He went ahead, to where the passage became tighter and more awkward to squeeze through, into a chamber at the end. The rest of us decided to turn back before this chamber as Mick's stature was rather too large for the tight bits. Needless to say, we kept out of the water on the way back! We then retraced our steps back into 'Salubrious Passage' and continued downstream, until we came to the end of the passage near 'The Crossroads'. The awkward, upwards, narrow, slippery, slot provided the others with some entertainment as I wriggled and squirmed most inelegantly to inch myself up it to reach 'The Crossroads'. However, I did manage it without any help! I could then watch the antics of the others as I sat comfortably above. That particular slot is difficult for most cavers to surmount elegantly, although Iain, coming up last, did it with nonchalant ease, born of much practice.

'The Crossroads' is aptly named and I led the way on to the right, then down over several large boulders to traverse a deep rift, at first on easy footholds and then on a small, muddied, ledge across 'President's Leap'. Here, there was a yawning drop below and the way on involved leaning out over the void, to use the far wall as support to avoid falling. As the years have passed, the ledge has become packed with the mud from cavers' boots and is no longer as flat as it was. One of these days I will take a hoe and clean it up again!

Everyone crossed 'President's Leap' with ease and we continued into the beautifully quiet, dry, musty-scented and well decorated tunnel of 'Selenite Passage'. We took our time here, admiring the formations and enjoying the easy going. Steve took some more photographs. At the end of this passage, we came to the 'Shattered Pillar' that seemed to support the roof of a small chamber, where there was a cross-road. To the right, was a route via a crawl, that could eventually be followed back to 'Gnome Passage'. In the past, I always took people this way to admire the 'Red Crystal' pool, but like several other formations, it had been sullied over the years by dust from its visitors' boots and did not warrant the effort.

After ensuring that Steve and Mick had made a note of the pillar as a useful route marker, we went left into a narrow rift passage that we thrutched along, until it dropped to a junction with the magnificent 'Cross Rift'. 'Cross Rift' is an obvious, unforgettable, landmark, well worth visiting. It is a high-roofed, narrow, rift that runs in a straight line for a considerable distance. The silence and gothic style of the rift gave it an ambience like that in a cathedral. We went left here, leaving the upper end of the rift to the right for exploration another day. The way here was fairly easy, until it ended in short, nicely lubricated, crawls with hardened mud floors that led into the area near 'The Maze'. We were soon able to stand up and quickly came to a deep hole, in a rift across the passage. The footholds that we had to use to step across this hole looked quite slippery. Ignoring the deep void below, everyone stepped carefully across this, without any problems.

On the other side, the passage was narrow and rose quite steeply, until we emerged back at the 'Crossroads'.

After catching our breath, we began the journey out. I had no trouble slipping down the awkward groove and I dropped easily into the end of 'Salubrious' passage again. From here, Steve and Mick led the way out to the entrance, with very few errors. At one decision point, Steve remarked how different the passages and key junctions looked when lit from the opposite direction! In a surprisingly short time, we were back at the 'Top Entrance' again. The gate opened from inside without a key, so we were soon sitting in the sun, on the stone wall near the entrance, while Iain enjoyed a smoke. The walk down to the SWCC cottages was easy, with delightful views across the valley below. As we strolled downhill, we chatted about all of the usual subjects under the sun. Back at the HQ, we checked in and then had the luxury of hot showers and cold beers or, in Heather's case, hot tea, afterwards. As we basked in the sun on the benches outside the cottages, sipping our drinks, we chatted with the other cavers who were staying there. We all felt pleasantly refreshed, and agreed that we were very lucky to have had such an enjoyable and interesting outing together. All of us looked forward to many happy returns to explore the countless possibilities inside the hills behind us.

Nowadays, in the age of the Internet, it is easy to cave vicariously. Anyone who is an arm-chair caver can repeat our round trip, or make alternative virtual tours of OFD, on the website: www.ogof.net for as long as it is actively maintained.

For anyone interested in the latest caving news in the area, the South Wales Caving Club website is: www.swcc.org.uk

19
The Living Cave

Once upon a time there was a cave that lived alone. Wrapped comfortably around its inner darkness, it could sense the outside world, but had no means of communicating its awareness of it. As far as it knew, it was the only sentient cave on the planet. Compared with the planet where it was born and lived, the cave was not so old. The planet had been born more than four billion years previously as a molten mass. It had slowly solidified and evolved chemically to form a surface that, after billions of years, could support life-forms. The cave was made of Carboniferous limestone, formed earlier on the planet's surface from marine sediments deposited from warm, shallow seas that were teeming with all sorts of life. This rock was about three hundred million years old. The rock had suffered all sorts of dreadful upheavals such as earthquakes, glaciations and rain-storms during its lifetime.

The cave was born by the action of water, long since departed, on the limestone rock. It was still subject to weathering, earth movement and invasion by animals of different sorts, some quite intelligent. As it overlooked the valleys and hills outside its entrance, it could sense their presence from vibrations in the surrounding rock and from the infra-red rays that bathed its outer surfaces. It had a long life ahead of it and spent its time just being a cave.

This story begins when the cave was dry enough to shelter a small group of bipeds. Before they arrived, it had been used by various quadrupeds for shelter and hibernation. The short, chestnut-haired bipeds discovered the cave on a hunting and gathering foray in the area. After sheltering from the rain, they explored its interior and eventually returned with their families. They used it as a home for many generations, lighting fires near the entrance and polluting the interior with discarded bones from their meals and rubbish. The cave did not like the heat and smoke, but could do nothing about it. This first group was evicted by a second group of bipeds. These had bigger heads, were less hairy and were taller than the first bipeds. The second group seemed to be more intelligent. They all wore the skins of animals that they had killed with their stone axes and bows and arrows.

Unfortunately, they lit fires, too. They also hacked away some of the loose bits of the cave and burnt it on large fires for some purpose of which the cave was unaware. They only stayed in the cave for a century or so and eventually left to set up homes and farms down in the valley, far away from the cave.

The cave lived alone for several more centuries, until it was visited by another set of bipeds that seemed to be quite human. These did not live in the cave, but rummaged and dug in its floor for artefacts and bones, seeking evidence of the previous occupants. They, too, disappeared eventually and the centuries rolled on, with occasional brief visits from small groups of bipeds with lights on their heads and large feet. Many years passed and the earth shook occasionally, making the cave tremble and crumble in places, but otherwise it stayed where it was, just being a cave.

The next visitors looked like humans, but were strongly constructed of some sort of artificial skin that glistened as they moved around. They were actually intelligent machines! They entered the cave to shelter from a group of super-human bipeds that was hunting them in flying machines that carried powerful weapons. The cave suffered serious damage from these weapons, that melted some of its rock when the two factions fought for supremacy. It was a blessing when they all went away, leaving most of the cave intact. The cave was left alone for a few billion years. Luckily, it was of no interest to the artificial intelligence that ruled the world in those times. The intelligent machines were more interested in exploring outer space for a suitable future refuge. The vibrations from these beings eventually ceased after another billion years.

The planet seemed to have been abandoned, but it became a great deal hotter. The grass and vegetation around the cave was burnt off and the area became an arid desert. Violent windstorms assailed the cave and dust blew inside it, choking the entrance. Nothing moved in the valley below, except the dust-devils and whirl-winds. The world seemed utterly life-less. Several billion years later still, the sky went a fiery red and the cave felt strong sunlight and infra-red rays beaming in without respite. The cave stood firm and alone, doing nothing except dream, happily unaware that the sun was evolving into a Red Giant. When the planet was swallowed by the rapidly expanding red sun, the cave gave its precious darkness back to the universe. Its ten billion year life ended and no-one noticed.

20
Caving Diaries

People have used diaries ever since cuneiform and hieroglyphics were invented. Diaries provide a reliable way of organising our lives between the past, the present and the future. Living in the present is reality, but the past and the future reside in our minds. Diaries are used to help us to recall past events and to plan our future.

There are basically two types of diary. The most common diary is used for the efficient management of time. It is used to book appointments and to plan the future. This sort of diary can also be used to check events that happened at particular times in the past, but without much detail. The other type of diary is used to record events for history, usually as a personal diary, to comment on events that have happened to the author. This latter type of diary may also provide some insight into the author and has often been used to prepare biographies of famous people. Pepys, George Bernard Shaw, Sir Walter Scott, Kafka, Kierkegaard, H.S.Truman, Lewis Carroll, Beatrix Potter and Virginia Woolf, were famous diarists, to name but a few. Many of us keep personal diaries, not so much for others to read, but for us to confide in. Such diaries enable us to look back at our past with some accuracy. Many cavers keep diaries to record their caving trips, equipment usage, and so on, for the same reason. A diarist has to be literate, of course. Writing is essential to compile a diary.

Writing was developed independently in Egypt and China, many thousands of years ago. The earliest Sumerian cuneiform inscriptions on clay tablets were made around 3000BC and the Neolithic peoples were using 'proto-writing' around 7000BC. Today, with electronic text processing and the Internet, there is an increasingly vast amount of writing, disseminated worldwide at the touch of a button. The on-line diaries and discussion sites, or 'Blogs' on the Internet, have evolved since the 1990's. There are now 'Multi-author Blogs' that are supported by the media, universities and other organisations. In 2012 there were at least seventy million 'Blog' sites. With so much electronic data, there is a risk it could be quickly lost and be too voluminous to study. Such 'Digital diaries' are more ephemeral than the old clay tablets, inscribed stones, vellum and paper. They are a sign of the rapidly changing and transitory nature of modern times. Anyone who keeps a diary in digital form should always print it as hard copy to ensure that, when the text processing system crashes, it is not irrecoverably lost!

It is interesting to study the investment of time and effort in diaries, particularly those that are kept as personal records and commentaries on events. Suppose that a diarist spends on average ten minutes a day writing a diary. In a year, this will amount to $365 \times 10/60 = 61$hrs work. In a lifetime of around 60 years, this will amount to 3660hrs, which is about 152 days, or about five months of work. If it takes half as long to read a diary as to write it, then a reader would need to spend at least two months reading it. Unless the diarist is someone famous, very few people would take the trouble to read their diary thoroughly if it took two months to do so! It makes one think that when we write personal diaries, we are doing it mainly for our own interest and not for posterity.

As well as diaries, there are many other ways that humanity has recorded events. The North American Indians used totem poles, for example. The most interesting to cavers, however, are the Magdalenian cave paintings. These were endowed with a magical touch, and reveal that the artists who made them were intelligent. Once writing had become common-place, travellers on exploratory expeditions kept a diary of events to enable them to write a full report of their findings on their return. The captains of ships on exploratory voyages, kept detailed logs and constructed maps to record their discoveries. Several well-educated and literate people wrote personal diaries, as has been mentioned already. Governments and local authorities collected information for tax and other purposes, such as the registers of birth and deaths. Commercial organisations kept accounts, annual reports and records of their business, too.

Nowadays, there are many archives of material recorded in diaries, or in other forms. Librarians manage these archives and store papers, books and other media, for retrieval by researchers. Modern historians have access to a wealth of documentation that can be used to describe and investigate past times. Ancient historians were not so well endowed and had to rely on scarce written works and oral information. Much of 'history' is coloured by the opinions and beliefs of the historians. This often makes it difficult to confirm exactly what happened in the distant past. Truth often lies in the eye of the beholder! History is often rewritten in the light of new material.

There is no fully authorised history of modern caving and potholing, as far as the author is aware. It would certainly be an interesting and profitable history if someone were to compile it. All of the caving clubs and organisations have records, newsletters, magazines, books and electronic data in their libraries, for an historian to consult. For many years, the British Cave Research Association has maintained a list of abstracts and reports that record scientific papers and discoveries. There have also been several books written by cavers that would be helpful to an historian, too. For example, the caving magazine "*Descent*" is an easily readable and reliable source of caving events, stories and discoveries that are not clouded by scientific jargon. The Internet is also a vast source of information that can be studied, using selective databases. Perhaps, in view of the foregoing comments about historians, it would be best if the historian were a caver. This raises an interesting point. It seems that most active cavers are sportsmen, scientists, engineers, or technologists. Historian cavers are as rare as chicken's teeth!

Many cavers use their diaries to plan ahead and reserve dates for trips and events organised by their club, or other caving organisations. A few cavers keep a proper record of their caving trips, especially those who use their own ropes and equipment. Those cavers who do keep a diary are in a position to add to the history of caving. On a practical note, it is important to have a robustly constructed diary in which to write, so that it can be safely stored. The author uses well-constructed, one page to a day, diaries, for example. Once these have been filled, they are stored in a strong chest of drawers. The author started his caving diaries in 1958 and has completed one for each year, so the drawers are rather full at the time of writing this book! Younger cavers would use a digital diary nowadays, requiring less space, but the problem of safe storage still remains. The most important thing is to write one's diary regularly so that it is always up-to-date.

Anyone researching the history of caving would have to glean the information available, written, digital, or verbal. If all else failed, the historian could interview the cavers themselves, particularly the older ones! Older cavers are rather like time-machines. They can re-live the past and can recall events that occurred over several decades. The value of their information will depend on when, where and how long, they went caving. Older cavers can transmit the oral tradition in the same way that the ancients did before writing was invented. Of course, you cannot always believe old cavers, even though they no longer wear animal skins, but eat cooked food and can read and write. They sometimes exaggerate the dangers that they overcame and make far too many jokes about caving to be believed!

Thistle Cave

21
Thistle Cave

Older cavers with grandchildren can have great pleasure in introducing them to caving. From the tender age of three, or four, boys and girls are usually interested in doing something different and slightly adventurous. A simple and interesting caving trip may just fit the bill for them! Depending on where they live, there are lots of caves suitable for youngsters to explore in Britain. Local cavers in any of the limestone regions, will be able to suggest where they are and which are suitable. Alternatively, the printed caving guides to the region will provide useful information. Since our family frequently visits Ingleton, the children have enjoyed caving from a very early age, as there is a good selection of caves suitable for them in the area.

Yordas and Jingling Cave in Kingsdale, Great Douk Cave in Chapel-le-Dale, Borrins Moor and the Long Churn Cave near Alum Pot, Thistle Cave and its parallel partner Runscar Cave at Ribblehead, have all proved very popular with them. Thistle and Runscar caves are easily accessible from the road and are particularly good as a first caving trip for youngsters. These two caves have additional advantages: Simple logistics, easy parking and an ice-cream and 'butty' van nearby for afterwards. However, because of these advantages, many groups come from far and wide to explore these caves, so they can sometimes be very busy!

Rather than describe one of these caves myself, I asked my granddaughter Clare to write up a trip that she did with her sister in Thistle Cave. Here it is:

Grandad Mum and Dad took me and Isabel into a cave called Thistle cave near the cottage at Ingleton. My Grandad likes to go into caves. He goes into lots of caves. Granny says he is too old to go in caves now but she says it keeps him happy. Grandad is my Mums Dad. When Mum was a girl he took her into lots of caves. Mum took me and Isabel into a big cave called Yordas when we were little and Isabel was scared. She thinks bears live in caves. Now I am seven and Isabel is four we can go into Thistle cave. We put on helmets and Mum fixed lights on the helmets because it is dark in caves. We put on our wellies as it is wet in caves. We walked across a moor to the cave that was very boggy. Mum carried Isabel over a bog as her wellies were too small. The cave was in a cliff up the hill. It was low down to get in. Grandad went in first. He had to crawl in. I went in next. Inside I could stand up. Mum came in with Isabel. There was a place to sit where we waited for Dad. Grandad checked the lights. He let me go first. I walked along the passage. It was damp and pretty. There was white stuff on the walls. There was a big hole in the wall at one place. Grandad said it was an oxbow. He said I could go inside it but I liked the walking passage better. We came to a deep pool and some water came inside my wellies. I got wet feet. Grandad carried Isabel across because her wellies were too small. Isabel got tired and she was a bit scared. Grandad told her there was a picnic chamber further on. Isabel likes picnics and was happy. I went on. It was a long way. The picnic chamber was big with a ledge to sit on. We sat down and Mum gave us some juice and chocolate. Dad took a photo of us. Granddad put all the things back in his bag and then I went round the corner. The cave went on. I went first until I saw some day light. I climbed up the rocks to get out. It was sunny outside. Grandad helped Isabel out. We saw a viaduct. Mum and Dad came out and we went back to the car where there was an ice cream van. Mum got some bacon buns for us to eat. It was good fun. I love caving. Clare

Runscar Cave
August 2012

22
The Old Man and the Cave

Once upon a time, an older caver was returning home from a day's walk across the moors. He stopped for a cigarette and sat on a convenient rock to smoke it. He lit the cigarette and dropped the dying match at his feet to stamp it out. However, as it touched the ground, he noticed that the smoke was blown by a draught coming out of the grass. He leant down and puffed some tobacco smoke at the spot. The draught blew the smoke upwards and seemed to be very strong. He pulled at the grass and heather to uncover the source of the draught. Underneath the heather, were lots of medium sized rocks and one or two large boulders that formed a choke, with a rock-face to one side. It looked a good place to dig for a new cave! He decided to return with a crow-bar and a rope to see what was under the choke.

The next day, he arrived early in the morning and set to work. The rocks and boulders were fairly easy to pull out and, by lunchtime, he had excavated a deep hole with a rock-face on one side and a jumble of rocks and boulders on the other. It looked quite promising, especially as the draught increased as he removed the constriction. He decided to get help and returned the next day with a couple of caving friends. They soon began to have trouble with the loose rocks and boulders, however. It was clear that they would have to put up supports, or scaffolding, to stop the rocks from falling into the main dig and entombing the workers. A few days later they returned and made the dig safe with scaffold poles, steel cables and thick planks of wood. By now the dig was several metres deep, so they fixed up a pulley system to lift rocks and other debris out to the surface. Over the weeks that followed, they dug deeper and deeper, but still had loose rocks and boulders below and no signs of a cave. As the weeks ran into months, the dig became deeper and deeper, with no breakthrough and his friends eventually decided to give it up.

He was somewhat disheartened by their decision, but decided that he would continue digging by himself. He worked on and off for several years without breaking through and the dig became so deep that he had to use his caving lamp at the bottom. The draught did not diminish, however and he thought that he could hear water flowing below the dig face. When he told his friends of this, they joined him again for a final push, but, after several days work, it came to nothing and they drifted away again. He refused to give up his struggle, however, and went once or twice a week to extend the dig and maintain the supports within it to prevent it from collapsing. The years passed quickly and still there was no sign of a breakthrough, but the dig was now in a well-defined tube. It looked like a proper pothole. Encouraged by this, his helpers returned, but after several weeks work, they gave up again. It really looked as if the dig would go on down forever!

After ten years of digging, the caver had aged considerably and was beginning to think that he would never have the strength and tenacity to achieve a breakthrough. Then, just as he was about to give up, one of the rocks in the dig fell through into empty space. He was through! He worked to clear more rocks and discovered that he could let them fall through rather than take them up to the surface. His friends returned once again when he told them what had happened. Together, they cleared the dig to the walls of the pothole. Unfortunately, all of the rocks that he had let fall, now blocked the way on! When they had cleared the fallen rocks out, they discovered that there were still more rocks below. The 'empty space' was not as large as he had thought! Once again the dig was full of rocks and digging had to continue. His helpers gradually drifted away and he was on his own again. Although he became tired more quickly, he did not give up his struggle with the rocky choke. He worked steadily away at the dig for another year and decided that he would give up when winter came. Then in the autumn, he broke through!

The way was open into a small rift, that led to a wider passage where he could stand up. He could hear the sound of a stream, too. The passage led to a junction with a large, well-decorated stream-way. Downstream, the passage ended in a sump. He waded upstream, marvelling at the beautiful stalactites hanging from the roof and the white, glossy stalagmites perched along the walls. He came to a chamber with clouds of straw stalactites in the roof and sparkling crystals on the floor and walls. It was the most beautiful cave he had ever seen! He felt so excited to have discovered it and wanted to explore further, but had to return as his light was running low. He was so elated as he began the long climb up to the surface that his tiredness seemed to vanish. He was very tired, nevertheless, and he slipped once or twice as he struggled up the scaffolding at the bottom of the shaft.

Unfortunately, in the last few months, he had skimped on the scaffolding and a careless move dislodged one of the supports at the bottom. As he climbed higher, he heard the rocks shifting and hastened upwards as the supports in the bottom of the shaft began to collapse. He was lucky to make it to the surface! Down below, the bottom of the shaft had filled with loose rock and debris again! He did not care though. He had seen the heaven that he had been seeking all of these years!

Needless to say, when he told his friends, they soon rallied round and helped him to clear the bottom of the shaft and stabilise it so that further exploration could continue. Unlike Hemingway's Santiago in 'The Old Man and The Sea', this Old Man had not only fought and caught his marlin, but brought it home as well!

23
The Caving Net

The caving net is a tremendous asset to every active caver. It spans the world and connects caving organisations, societies and clubs as well as individual cavers, by using many different means of communication, including the Internet. Any caver in the caving net becomes part of an international community. The older cavers, who have built up their contacts over many years, often play a significant role in the caving net, repairing breakdowns and opening up new lines of communication. Before describing it further, it may be interesting and instructive to explain exactly what a 'Net' is and how I came to learn about it.

I first heard the word 'Net', when I was at grammar school and had to join the 'Combined Cadet Force' (CCF). This was compulsory with no exceptions. Every Monday, I had to go to school in army uniform and boots, so that I could spend the afternoon learning how to 'drill', map read, shoot a rifle, strip a Bren gun, perform 'section in attack' and do numerous disciplined military activities. The CCF was a pleasant diversion from lessons, even if tiresome and onerous on occasions! Once I had passed all of the preliminary tests, been to cadet camp and elevated to the rank of lance-corporal, I was able to join the 'Signals Unit'. This was really fun! We were taught how to use wireless sets that could be carried on our backs and how to set up the 'Net' that connected them. We even had to speak a special language when on 'Net': "Able, Baker, Charlie, Dog… How do you read me? Roger! Wilco. Out!" and so on. Once we were competent, we were encouraged to practise using the sets around the school grounds, even out of CCF time. For example; we monitored the cross-country race and helped with orienteering exercises. I found radio fascinating and learnt as much about it as I could. I even made myself a crystal set at home.

Suddenly, it was time to leave school! I was tested and deemed fit enough, so now had to do my National Service. This was compulsory with no exceptions, too! With my CCF background and an interest in radio, I chose to go into The Royal Signals. At first, I thought that I had made a dreadful mistake! The 2nd. Signals Training Regiment

(2TR) at Catterick Camp gave me an awful shock. It was an incredibly tough and painful initiation into the army by specially trained disciplinarians with very loud voices, all backed up by military law. The basic idea seemed to be to wear us down so that we would submit to army discipline, regardless of who we were and where we came from. I rapidly learned my first lesson, one of many that I learned in the army. They lined us up for the first day's drill and told us to step forward if we had been in the CCF. Naively thinking that I could avoid drill, I stepped forward, along with three others. We were told to fall out and summarily marched to a horribly vile and smelly tip behind the cookhouse. Here, we spent the drill period cleaning it up! From then on I never volunteered again!

Even worse followed! I discovered that I had been designated an OR1 (*Other Ranks 1*) and had to go for officer training! This was even harder and more fatiguing than 2TR. For drill, we even had sharp bayonets that could cut one's fingers instead of blunt pencil ones! The assault course was ten times harder, too! I passed all of the relevant tests until, finally, I had to go before the War Office Selection Board (WOSB) down at Sandhurst. For the first time in my life I failed something... I was failed as 'Too immature'. "How insulting", I thought! I was nineteen and not at all immature!

This time, however, I was in luck. I had escaped the net of office! I was selected to become an 'X3: Heavy Radio Technician' and sent on a course at the 4th. Signals Training Regiment (4TR), also at Catterick. The aim of the course was to teach me to operate and maintain the Royal Signals' heavy radio networks on the battlefield and in sites, protected from nuclear attack, all around the world. Here I was taught all about the transmission and reception of signals by radio waves. I learnt about amplitude modulation, frequency modulation, independent sideband modulation, double super-heterodyne and triple diversity reception, voice and printer systems, cypher, power generation and aerial design. I learned how to select the best aerial, from an array of rhombic aerials that pointed in different directions, to transmit either way around the world, depending on the forecasts for the Appleton and Heaviside ionised layers overhead. With all of the various bits and pieces, signal diversity, environments and different locations, the word 'Net' became an important part of my vocabulary. It was not until many years later, when computers became freely available that I realised how important such 'Nets' were. The development of packet switching, e-mail and the Internet, revealed the true power of a 'Net'. We are all interconnected nowadays!

The word 'Networking' has been much used, outside its birthplace in communications technology, to describe social interactions in the human environment. 'Social Networks' before the Internet relied on education, schooling, religion, professional organisations, political parties, clubs, cliques and suchlike, for their construction and maintenance. These networks were also held together by rules such as 'rites of passage', formal meetings, journals, personal dress and etiquette. Any member of the network who broke the rules would be 'Black-balled', or ostracised. It was usually difficult for outsiders to gain access to these networks and still is in some cases. Nevertheless, individual success heavily depended on developing good social networks. You had to drink at the right pub if you wanted promotion!

The caving net is a much more friendly and welcoming network, but websites and pubs do play a prominent part in getting cavers together. There are certain rites of passage to join some clubs, but, in general, anyone who is really keen on caving can obtain access to a wide variety of contacts that can share and augment his, or her, particular caving interests. Every country has its own caving organisation that can be contacted via its website. In the UK, all of the established caving clubs have websites and there are regional organisations with websites, too. The British Caving Association (BCA) that includes The British Cave Research Association (BCRA), is the mainstay of British caving and the best point of entry into the caving network. If you are familiar with Venn diagrams, then these two bodies would be at the centre, with all of the subject groups, 160 registered clubs, cave rescue organisations, charitable bodies and other links connected into them. All of this is fairly formal, however, as the caving net exists widely and most strongly at the personal level, developing by word-of-mouth and the shared experiences of individuals.

Cavers have good memories of friends and caving companions that are continually refreshed at the caving meets, meetings, parties and annual reunions of their caving clubs. Most older cavers will have belonged to several caving clubs during their caving career, especially if they have moved house several times, or travelled abroad. There are many well-known caving clubs that have lasted for decades and are still very active. There were 160 caving clubs registered with the BCA in 2012, for example. Nevertheless, a few clubs fall by the way-side, or unite with larger clubs, depending on age, politics and social changes. The South West Essex Technical College Caving Club (SWETC) is an interesting case in point, as it contributed significantly to the caving net, with many ex-members prominent in BCRA, regional caving clubs and other organisations.

The SWETC Caving Club started at the South West Essex Technical College in 1958. However, when the college was re-named Waltham Forest Technical College in 1967, the caving club retained its original title as it had become well-known as such. In 1970, there was another educational system re-organisation and the college became part of the North East London Polytechnic. The continuous changes to the UK educational system recall the Roman centurion's comment: *"We trained hard, but it seemed that every time we were beginning to form into teams, we were re-organised."* Yet another re-organisation occurred and the college moved to the University of East London, Walthamstow precinct. The club had traditionally recruited from the surveying students, but when the central building in Walthamstow ceased to be part of the university, the students became based in lots of different locations around east London. This made communication difficult and the SWETC ceased to exist as a college based club in 1981. During all of this educational upheaval, however, the club kept caving actively and remained a coherent group of cavers that met together regularly to keep the SWETC Net going. In 1979, the key club members held an anniversary meeting that was attended by more than forty old SWETC members. From then on, an annual reunion has been held every year. Of course, even though the older members refused to get old and deemed themselves to be not as old as their age implied, the amount of active caving done by ex-club members reduced considerably. However, their offspring boosted attendance, so the reunions were always well attended. For example, the 50th Anniversary was attended by nearly a hundred old SWETC members. It just shows how cavers do not give up on their networks even when their club has disappeared!

The caving net is forever changing, as new cavers enter it and older cavers leave. When an older caver dies, the news is transmitted very quickly around the caving net, especially if the caver has made a significant contribution to the caving community. The funeral provides an opportunity for those attending to celebrate the life of the caver and to give condolences to his, or her, family and friends. Such funerals also provide a great opportunity for reunions of older cavers who had left the scene, or moved away from their roots. The loss of a caver is a loss for everyone in the caving community. The caving net, as well as providing communication between cavers as individuals, also engenders the spirit of caving and long may it continue.

24
Giant's Hole

Giant's Hole, near Castleton in Derbyshire, has an archetypical cave entrance with a stream flowing into it. The ancients could easily have believed that it housed a giant! The cave has been known for many years and has been explored to a depth of over four hundred feet (128m.). With about three kilometres of natural passages, it is a popular venue for cavers of all abilities, from beginners to experienced cavers. It is a particularly enjoyable venue for the older caver, too.

My first visit to the cave was during my National Service, when I was a complete novice caver. In retrospect, it was a visit that should have put me off caving forever, but, for some unknown reason it never did! In those days, after the large entrance passage, the roof lowered right down to water-level, leaving only a small airspace. I was told that this was a 'duck' and that I would have to get wet if I wanted to carry on into the cave. We were only wearing our army 'Long John's' under our overalls, so passing the duck was a very cold experience! Worse was to follow! Further on we came to a series of dams in the passage. I saw that the dams had open holes at the bottom to let the water out. Ahead, the passage was filled to the roof with water. I learned that this was called a 'sump' and that we would have to bale it out if we wanted to pass through it into the rest of the cave. There were various old pots, a leaky bucket and some plastic bags and pieces of wood to block up the dams, lying there for this purpose. After plugging the holes in the dams, we started baling out the water into them, even using our helmets to speed things up. After lots of hard work, the dams were almost all filled up, but the airspace was still insufficient for us to risk trying to pass through. Eventually, by common consent, we abandoned the project and left the cave, soaking wet and cold, to get changed and go somewhere else.

Fortunately, since then, these watery obstacles have been removed, following an abortive attempt by one of the farmers to create a show-cave. Unless the cave is in flood, it is now a straightforward walk in the stream-way as far as a blasted passage to the left, that avoids the obstacles. The way on is then relatively dry, with a few slippery descents and some stooping, until it arrives at the spacious and well-decorated 'Base Camp Chamber'. The main stream re-appears here on the right, as a noisily splashing cascade after rain, or running along the wall to fall as a raggedy curtain in dry summer days. Beginners and children are always glad to be able to stand on firm ground here and to walk around looking at the formations. It is possible to climb back upstream for a short way and there is also a climb up into the roof near the cascade, to a small passage that is well decorated and often used for beginner's trips. The way on, however, is to follow the stream as it weaves its way past some beautiful flowstone benches, under the climb to 'Boss Aven' and then beneath a white, flowstone-covered aven; a shaft that enters from high above. Past the formations, the passage lowers and the walls and floor are dark and unreflective, which generate a gloomier atmosphere. The sound of a waterfall can soon be heard and, in a few yards, the stream pours over several small landings until it crashes noisily down 'Garlands Pitch'. For children and older folk, this is usually the end of their visit. Their guide would usually fix a safety rope across the passage to allow them to clip into it and look down the pitch, before leading them back to have a picnic in 'Base Camp Chamber'.

'Garlands' pitch is only thirty feet deep, but usually wet. When in flood, it is not advisable to descend here, but very exciting to see. The pitch can be descended on a rope or by an 'Electron' ladder with a safety rope. At the bottom, there is a pebbly floor where you can usually keep out of the spray and wait for the others to descend. Here, the stream flows into a narrow, meandering, rift passage called 'The Crab Walk', due to the fact that you have to inch sideways along it as it is rather tight in places. From here on, there are several interesting routes that can be explored, depending on your ability and fitness.

An interesting route for older cavers is to continue downstream until there is an enlargement of the passage and a small cascade. There is an easy climb up to the left into a muddy passage above the stream. The passage bends to the right and emerges above 'The Crab Walk' again. Here, you need to straddle across the void and then carefully traverse around a right-hand bend, high above the stream-way until you reach easy footholds again. There is then a fairly easy climb up into the roof to a flat floor. A low, wet, well-decorated, crawl then leads through to the top of a pretty flowstone cascade. Slither down this to the bottom. There is a tight-looking, calcite-covered slot in the rift to your left, facing up the flowstone cascade that you just came down. The 'Eye-hole' may present a problem for very large people, but the slot is fairly easy to squeeze through on one's side, using handholds to keep your body from slipping down and jamming in the tighter parts. There is also a minor problem on the other side of the slot. You need to maintain a level height in the rift. As there are virtually no holds you must apply pressure with shoulders and knees against the walls to help you through until you can use the slippery footholds further on. A final wriggle upwards leads to a roomy passage high above the 'The Crab Walk' where the stream can be seen glinting far below. Although there is a deep rift in the floor, you can progress along the passage, straddling the drop with your feet on small footholds on each side. However, do not use the black chert footholds as they are prone to snap off unexpectedly!

There are several ways down the rift into 'The Crab Walk' here, negotiable with or without a rope, but the way on leads across to a series of well-decorated passages. The passage soon narrows and is blocked by flowstone with a beautiful little letter-box squeeze on your stomach into a pool of standing water. The passage the other side of this is smallish and covered with flowstone in places. Here, you have to move sideways as the way on is rather like a smaller version of 'The Crab Walk. The passage soon enlarges and you come to the best formations in the cave. Stalactites, stalagmites and flowstone bosses gleam brightly everywhere. There are a couple of pleasant small chambers to explore up climbs to the side of the passage, too. After the decorations, the passage becomes smaller and several crawls follow until a low bedding plane duck called 'The Giant's Windpipe' is reached.

If you wished to continue to the bottom of the cave, you would have to wriggle through this duck, keeping your nose and mouth as near to the ceiling as possible in order to breathe! The route after the duck is via a complex of passages climbs, crawls and pitches that lead eventually to the final sump in East Passage over four hundred feet below the level of the entrance. This is a superb sporting trip that takes an hour or more for fit cavers with the proper equipment. Then, after a breather or a photo, you would have to fight your way back out to the surface. In spite of this superb attraction, at this point, the duck may not seem to be worth the effort and cavers over seventy usually turn back!

Back above the rift again, it is possible to look down and locate an easy route to chimney down to 'The Crab Walk'. Alternatively, if there are beginners in the party, there is a belay for anchoring a rope so that they can abseil down instead of chimneying. From then on it is only a few minutes of sidling upstream in 'The Crab Walk' to return to 'Garlands' again.

In addition to the routes just described, there is another route in the cave that is a more serious undertaking, but only for fit and relatively thin cavers. From the passages on the other side of 'The Giant's Windpipe' there is a connection to Oxlow Caverns through a long, very tight and awkward crawl that is sometimes impassable when parts of it fill with water. Once through the notorious crawl and in the Oxlow system, it is possible to exit via a series of pitches, if they have been rigged previously, to the Oxlow entrance. In addition to this, it is also possible to take a route from Oxlow Caverns into to the nearby Maskill Mine. The depth from the Maskill entrance to East Canal in Giant's Hole is six hundred and ninety three feet (211m.), so this is one of the most significant traverses in Britain.

Giant's Hole provides a wide variety of enjoyable and interesting routes for all levels of caving expertise. For example, one summer evening, I went into Giant's Hole with several members, beginners and potential members of my local caving club, the Crewe Climbing and Potholing Club (CCPC). The weather had been fine for a week, so the water level was quite low. This enabled us to organise several different trips into the system to suit the various abilities and expertise of the participants. There were about twenty of us so, the versatility of Giant's hole was exploited to the full!

One team descended 'Garlands Pitch', continued down 'The Crab Walk' to 'The Eating House' and returned via 'The Wind-pipe' and the 'High Level' series. Another team climbed 'Boss Aven' to do some maintenance work and admire the formations. I went down 'Garlands Pitch' and climbed up to visit the high level series. The beginners did not descend Garlands, but explored the side passages off 'Base Camp Chamber'. The rest spent their time photographing each other and the formations. By the time that we were all back on the surface, it was dark. Luckily, there was just enough time to visit 'The Wanted Inn' for refreshment. Unfortunately, we discovered that the pub was due to be closed permanently that week. This was another sad example of the erosion of the local pub culture. Fortunately, for cavers at least, in spite of the changes in the world of commerce and society, Giant's Hole will outlast them all!

25
Silence

Silence is the canvas on which music is painted. "Silent? Ah, he is silent! That man's silence is wonderful to listen to." *Thomas Hardy.* "Silence is deep as Eternity; speech is shallow as time" *Thomas Carlyle.* Silence has inspired many poets, prophets and writers through the ages. Nowadays it is becoming rarer, however. Silence must be sought, wherever it may be found. This particularly applies to caves. Most active caves are naturally quite noisy due to running or dripping water. In hot climates, some caves have such a fierce draught that there is wind noise. Silence is found in the dry fossil passages high above the active stream-ways, or in isolated passages and dry caverns that are no longer active. Mines and lava tube caves are mostly silent. Silence gives an atmosphere to any cave, or mine and can inspire one to pause and think before returning to the noisy world outside.

"So, what is silence?" You may ask. "Silence is defined as the absence of noise." I would reply. "So, what is noise, then?" You may ask, thinking that you are being smoke-screened...

"The Oxford Dictionary defines noise as any sound, especially undesired sound." I would reply.

We are fortunate that modern technology gives us excellent access to desired sound, such as music, poetry, plays and literature. However, in the world at large, unwanted sound, or noise, is everywhere. We are bombarded continually by all sorts of media. In the open air we hear ghetto blasters, traffic, pneumatic drills, aeroplanes and ambulances. On our TV screens we are deluged with images and dramas that are often noisy and violent. Noisy politicians use obfuscation and 'spin' to deceive us. In the press, reporting is often inaccurate and sensationalized 'noise', rather than a quietly balanced viewpoint. Much of the noise in the media is a distraction. Besides, it is often generated by celebrities who have no knowledge of the caving world anyway!

These definitions of 'Silence' and 'Noise' are somewhat limited. Only audio/visual communications have been considered. For a more general appraisal, we need to include other means of communication such as electro-magnetic radiation, touch, smell, taste and body language. (*If telepathy were proven to be real, then this, too, could be another source of communication.*) A more general definition of 'Silence' is that it is when no signal is received. (*Radio Silence for example*) In this context, wanted noise is the signal that bears information and unwanted noise is the interruption of the signal with unwanted information.

Communication Theory uses the parameter "Q" to quantify the quality of signal reception. Q quantifies the relationship between the Selectivity and the Sensitivity of the receiver. *For example:* A very sensitive radio set can pick up everything over a broad band of frequencies, but the signals will be too many and too strong to obtain a good specific signal, because it gets drowned out. If the set is too selective, it can tune in to only one signal, but may have difficulty in finding it among all of the 'noise'. "Q" measures the ability of a receiver to obtain a clearly interpretable signal with no 'noise'.

There are other aspects of 'Silence' that may be pertinent:

• In scientific terms, absolute silence may be similar to '*Absolute Zero*', '*Zero Risk*', and travelling at the speed of light. These are all theoretical concepts that cannot be achieved in our physical world.

• The universe is filled with the residual radiation from the 'Big Bang', so absolute silence is unattainable as a consequence.

• Silence is a vital element in life, for heightened perception, meditation and relaxation.

There are many subtle and obvious sounds and experiences to be had in caves. We only need to be able to observe and understand them. The main problem is that this requires time and the ability to perceive them. There is so much noise and hurry in some caving trips, that many delightful phenomena are easily rushed past, or drowned out by excited chatter. In the vernacular of this chapter, cavers should try and develop a '*High Q*', both in the caves and in communicating with the vast and varied emissions of information above the ground in the modern world.

Alan Plater's TV play '*The Beiderbecke Connection*' provides an amusing example of how a message can be lost. The play was transmitted without piped laughter, but with delightful jazz as background music. At the end of the play, the main character stated forcefully: "*There's only two sorts of people. Those who hear the music and those who don't*". At another point, exasperated by one of the other characters, the hero bewailed: "*You only have to listen!*"

The analogies provided in this chapter are only simple models. They may provide some insight, but can become misleading if they are overextended. It does seem clear, however, that mind-ful perception is not easy in the modern world. Each individual needs to become highly tuned to his environment and give time and space for silence in which to perceive it. Finding silence, however, does not have to be physical and external. It can be a matter of personal disposition. Some people can be silent and alone in a noisy crowd. Silence may be found within ourselves. For example, Quaker Meetings are held on a basis of silence and the congregation attempt to listen to the promptings of their hearts to achieve a unity in the presence of their faith.

The older cavers will probably have more time for this sort of philosophizing than the younger ones. They have to wait around in caves more often, while the youngsters rig the pitches, or go off exploring side passages. Hopefully, they can find a comfortable place to sit that is dry and quiet. Also, older cavers turn their lamps off when they are at rest to conserve their batteries. This provides a good opportunity to observe silence in the darkness and to meditate. It is quite surprising how quickly time passes when such opportunities are taken. Suddenly they all return, full of energy and excitement and you have to get up and start caving again!

26
Caving in The Mendips

My memories of caving in the Mendips include hitching to the old premises of the Wessex Cave Club at Hillgrove and getting very wet and cold in the local caves, in spite of this being over fifty years ago. Caving in those days seemed to be truly exciting and always a source of wonder to me. We always seemed to emerge late at night, wet, muddy, thirsty and hungry, with a hectic rush to get to 'The Hunter's' before closing time! In my youth, the Mendips were my nearest caving region and I frequently hitched lifts there to go caving. The cave system names of Swildon's, Cuthbert's, Eastwater, Stoke Lane Slocker and 'G.B.' together with 'Maine's Barn' and 'The Hunter's Inn' are always a nostalgic reminder of my youth.

After moving to Cheshire, I rarely went there except for special occasions such as a club meet or a birthday party, so soon I lost touch with the scene. In fact, I have not been there since I retired and that was fourteen years ago! After the age of seventy, the general tightness and wetness of the systems ceased to be an attraction for me and I abandoned any thought of going there again. However, when I read Pete Glanville's excellent article in '*Descent No.229*' about the history of Reservoir Hole and the discovery of the huge chamber, called 'The Frozen Deep', in 2012, I revised my opinion.

Reservoir Hole is in Cheddar Gorge and there were many digs there over the years that advanced its length and promise. It always seemed to be a rather arduous and muddy cave to me and as access was controlled, it was never on my wish-list. However, Pete Glanville and his friends launched a sustained attack to extend the system in 2008 that continued until the final breakthrough to 'The Frozen Deep' in 2012. I quickly made enquiries and soon found that Chris Binding was a guide and could organise visits in the season.

However, Chris, having caved with me recently, reckoned that I would not enjoy such a trip. I was easily, perhaps too easily, put off the idea. At seventy five, my confidence was waning, but I felt sure that I could do the trip, given enough time and patience. However, this is where the rot sets in! I decided that I really ought to take a nostalgic visit the Mendips and go caving, even if my original target would have to wait. The large chamber in 'GB' seemed a second best to the vast void in 'The Frozen Deep' and would certainly be easier.

I began to plan the visit with considerable enthusiasm. That is where the rot really began to flourish! There is no doubt that inertia and apathy are dreadful afflictions that become almost endemic in the older caving population. They have to be fought off strenuously! I began to struggle. Since I was writing this book at the time, I thought that there would have to be a chapter about caving in the Mendips. This trip could provide the solution! I have fond memories of 'GB' and felt I could write an amusing and interesting chapter about a visit there as an older caver. I contacted Keith, Aubrey and Chris to try and fix a suitable date. I quickly ran into problems, mainly of my own making.

Before retiring, I always dreamed of the life after work when I would be the master of my own time. I imagined the joy of being completely free to wander around the world, walking, climbing, caving, eating, drinking and generally enjoying myself with my friends. As mentioned earlier in this book: 'Anyone can dream!' A dream it was. I quickly discovered that my diary became just as full as it did when I was in work. Also, my younger friends still working had the same constraints as I had had and these now constrained me, too. Once most of them had retired, they had the same problem. Anyway, returning to my trip to Somerset: My diary was very full with holidays abroad, family engagements, theatre trips, club trips, medical appointments, garden chores, lectures and so on. I also had an objective to finish this book by the end of the summer. On top of that I wanted to walk up Carnedd Llewellyn before my arthritis got any worse and get in another caving trip in the Pyrenees as well, if possible. It became apparent that there was no way that I could go to Somerset until October at the earliest!

It was quite obvious that I could not visit Mendip in time to write up a caving trip for my book. I decided I would go there later in the year and have an enjoyable trip without writing it up. This *mañana* process can be helpful in the short term, but when you are an older caver, other issues and opportunities can make the original objective disappear altogether! One might console oneself that, living in harmony with the *Tao* is something to be sought, but, if the way does not pass through the Mendips, then so be it! To be perfectly honest, I have been doing this procrastination for several years with proposed trips to Mendip! So, there is the lesson! If you want to do something when you are over seventy: Do it as soon as you can or you'll never do it!

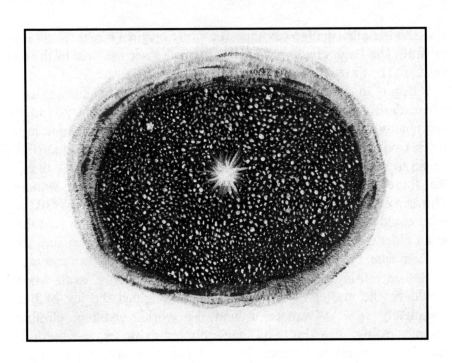

27
The Dreem

Once upon a time there lived a Dreem. The Dreem inhabited the vast morphological fields of the universe, along with others of its kind. It was very, very, large, but insubstantial, as it was totally composed of energy quanta. It survived by feeding on the morphological energy from intelligent life-forms, with whom it was symbiotic. The Dreem did not harm its hosts, but instilled them with dreams and ideas to improve their lives. Since there were so few intelligent life-forms in its universe, it spent much of its time seeking replacements for hosts that had expired.

One millennium, the Dreem discovered a remote galaxy that contained a medium-sized star with a habitable planet. The Dreem was in luck! The planet was teeming with intelligent life-forms that radiated morphological energy! However, there was a minor problem. Several others of its kind were farming there already. Fortunately there were enough life-forms to go round, so the Dreem's future energy supply could be secured for some time.

The Dreem spent a few decades investigating the intelligent life-forms available in order to select hosts that had the most morphological energy for its needs. It discovered that the life-forms burnt their energy fiercely and quickly. In comparison with the Dreem's time-frame, their lives were extremely fleeting, too. Unlike some of its previous hosts, these life-forms only lived for a few decades! Luckily, there were lots of them, but it was clear that the Dreem would have to find new hosts every few decades!

Undeterred by the problems of sharing hosts with such short life-spans, the Dreem decided to feed there for the few billenia remaining before the star became extinct. Like its fellow Dreems, it aimed to improve the lives of its hosts, especially if it resulted in them having longer lives. The Dreem soon selected several hosts on the planet that were satisfactory, but as it studied them, it was apparent that there was a great variety of host available.

The Dreem also made a surprising discovery. Some of the life-forms were aware of its presence! This phenomenon surprised the Dreem, especially when one of the potential hosts that it was examining suddenly reacted with a message. "Hello!" the host transmitted. The Dreem was amazed and quickly (*It took a year!*) replied, "Who are you?" There was an immediate and incredibly strong response: "I'm a caver! Who are you?" The Dreem had never encountered such a host before. It replied with the message "Hello! What's a caver?" Eventually the life-form received this message and parried with a reply. "You haven't told me who you are yet!" The Dreem took some time to construct and morph a message back. In fact, this task took it three or four decades. Unfortunately the host had expired before it arrived, so the Dreem did not get an answer to its question. Like all of its kind, the Dreem was very inquisitive. "I'll have to try and find another, younger one!" It thought to itself.

So watch out cavers! There's a Dreem out there looking for you!

28
The Ancient Caver

Not far from the South Wales Caving Club premises is a pub called 'The Ancient Briton'. This set me thinking. As it is a popular refreshment centre for the countless cavers who live and visit in the region, it ought to be called 'The Ancient Caver'. There are not many ancient cavers about nowadays, but there are quite a lot of older cavers, many of whom drink in 'The Ancient Briton'. The exact difference between an older caver and an ancient one may not be determined precisely on the basis of age or appearance. It may be that the oldest caver whom you know seems ancient, but it would very much depend on how old you were yourself. My grandchildren are quite sure that I am ancient, for example!

The oldest caver that I know is over ninety years of age and still goes caving occasionally, so cannot be strictly regarded as ancient. In my opinion he is a perfect example of how to keep an interest in caving, regardless of age. I first met Bill Varnedoe when I visited the United States of America in 1981. In those days, Bill was an active caver and very busy in the local community as a Fire Chief. He and his wife Louise were really hospitable and they welcomed many visiting cavers to their home during the International Caving Congress, held in Kentucky that summer of 1981. They invited Dilys, Catherine and me to come and stay with them in their house, on Green Mountain, outside Huntsville, when we were en route for Florida in that year. We spent a most enjoyable long weekend with them and were sad when we had to leave. Bill organised some interesting caving trips for us. He introduced us to several members of the Huntsville Grotto, who took me vertical caving locally. He also took us to visit the National Speleological Society Headquarters and library in Huntsville. We were very impressed with the extensive database of local caves and pits that he had developed and was updating continually. Over the years, we kept in touch regularly. In 1986, we met whilst I was caving at Matienzo. Bill and Louise visited there after attending the International Caving Congress held at Barcelona. In 1992, Bill and Louise came to visit us when his World War II 385th. Bomb Group celebrated its fiftieth anniversary in England. We went caving in the Peak District and Bill gave a very interesting talk on his war-time experiences to local cavers and residents. We still keep in touch regularly by e-mail and snail mail. Bill's life story and caving career are full of interest and would occupy a book, but I have selected a few exploits that I thought seemed germane to the philosophy of this chapter:

B-17 Flying Fortress

In World War II, Bill was in his twenties. He joined the war effort as a B-17 bomber navigator and navigated a B-17 across the Atlantic to Britain. He then navigated it on twenty six combat missions, bombing strategic targets in Germany. After surviving the war, he became an Electrical Engineer and moved to Huntsville in 1952, where he worked on rocket research. Louise, his wife, was a rocket engineer who worked on major space projects. Eventually he worked for NASA on the project to put a man on the Moon.

When Bill first moved to Huntsville he drove around the area surrounding his home to become familiar with it. One day, he spotted a cave entrance and took a flashlight to explore inside so that he could see what a cave looked like. He was immediately hooked and has been a caver ever since!

In America, the national caving organisation is The National Speleological Society (NSS). The NSS charters local caving clubs that are called Grottos. Since there were none in the Huntsville area, Bill founded the Huntsville Grotto with a group of friends. The Huntsville Grotto eventually became one of the largest Grottos in the NSS and was on the leading edge in the development and pioneering of single rope techniques (SRT).

Shortly after Bill founded the Huntsville Grotto, he went on a caving expedition locally and a young girl, whom Bill did not know, was invited as a guest. Several weeks later, when Bill was down at Cape Canaveral for a Redstone Rocket shoot, he went into town for his supper and noticed the girl sitting alone at a table in the restaurant. He went over, sat down and started a conversation with her. He was surprised to discover that she was an engineer who was down for the same Cape Canaveral shoot as he was. One thing led to another and they started dating regularly, frequently on caving trips. By the next Fall, they got married and, at the time of writing, have been together for 57 years!

Bill caved across America and in several countries overseas, but his main caving career has been in North Alabama, where he was chief of the local Cave Rescue Unit for twenty five years. As he became older, he took more interest in other aspects of caving such as photography, climbing techniques and climbing gadgets. He enjoyed inventing new and improved headlamps, too. In 1998, the NSS awarded him its highest award; The William J. Stephenson Award. This award endowed him with Life Membership. Bill, like all old cavers, has had to accommodate to the problems of age, as an e-mail from him in 2013 explains:

"Time has taken a toll on my body. I can no longer cave alongside the young healthy bucks. As I aged, my caving interest gradually shifted from pure exploration and long gruelling trips to other aspects of caving. When I passed 85 or 86 years old, I really slowed down and began doing research. Among my restrictions to more active caving are a 50% blockage which restricts my energy and efforts; my macular degeneration which makes seeing in dark places very difficult and my vertigo balance problems which makes cave negotiations perilous. It didn't help that I had a tractor accident recently that injured my back. My sole caving trip this year was to take an archaeologist into Turkey Cave, a cave that has Native American petroglyphs deep in the dark zone of the cave. Chuck Lundquist, my caving buddy, and I found these animal art depictions many years ago and brought them to the

attention of the archaeological community. The cave is not big, only about 600 feet long and is mostly tight crawling. That suits me – this old man can't *fall if I'm already on my belly!! The difficulty of getting to the petroglyphs in total darkness by crawling is actually one reason that they are especially valuable anthropologically."*

Very few cavers continue to cave past the age of seventy. Norbert Casteret, the famous French caver, was still actively caving at sixty, but his caving diminished until he passed the final sump aged ninety. Peter Harvey, who opened up Ogof Ffynnon Ddu in South Wales, continued active caving until he was well into his eighties. Several other well-known cavers have similar histories, but my old friend Bill is the only one who competes in the over nineties field at present. One of these days he will become ancient, but not just yet!

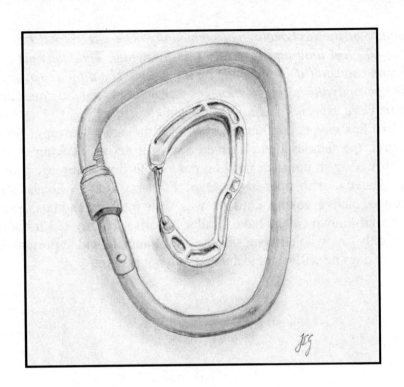

29
"Last of the summer wine."

Titan, the deepest underground shaft in Britain (*141.5m.*), is a magnet for many cavers. For those over seventy, especially those with arthritis, it is quite a challenge! I had wanted to descend it ever since an entrance from the surface had been dug successfully. I had specially reconnoitred the route as far as 'Colostomy Crawl' from 'The Treasury' in Peak cavern and through 'The Trenches' to confirm that I could exit via Peak Cavern if necessary. However, if possible, I wanted to complete the trip with an easier exit from Speedwell Mine. Luckily for me, Ralph Johnson had promised to fix a trip for me with an exit via Speedwell for my seventy-fifth birthday. So, along with a very good turn-out of Crewe cavers, I went to Castleton on an autumn Sunday to collect my birthday present.

More than twenty club members went underground that day. Whereas most of the cavers entered through the huge entrance of Peak Cavern to explore the system, five of us older club members went up the hill to Hurdlow to go down Titan and come out via Speedwell.

Someone jokingly remarked that seeing us preparing for our trip was just like an episode of '*The Last of the Summer Wine*', with no points for identifying '*Compo*', '*Cleggie*' or, '*Foggy*'!

Following the motto "*Be Prepared*", I had started preparations a fortnight beforehand. I bought a new '*wire-gate*' carabiner to use with my short '*cows-tail*' to make the free-hanging change-over on Titan easier than with my ancient hook-like one. I tested this out in the garage, hanging on a rope from a beam, to simulate a free-hanging bolt change. The Saturday before the trip, I took a 50mg Diclofenac tablet with breakfast, lunch and dinner and another at Sunday breakfast to lubricate my arthritic knees. As an older caver, it is sensible to take every precaution before going caving.

As usual, the club rendezvous was at the TSG 'Chapel' in Castleton at 0900 hrs. Adrian Pedley had rigged Titan on the Saturday and Jenny Drake had agreed to de-rig it Sunday, in the wake of us older cavers. Ralph arrived first to organise the documentation and logistics. I arrived at about the same time and was lucky enough to find a free parking place for my car. (*I would later use my car to give Ralph a lift back to his four-by-four parked at the end of the track leading to the fields near the top entrance*). Sharon Brandwood arrived shortly afterwards, and Jenny arrived later in her super-car. Once the logistics, gear and clothing had been sorted, Ralph drove Sharon and me up the lane to the fields near the entrance shaft in his four-by-four. Just as we were leaving Castleton, 'Steve' Knox and Paul Nixon drove up behind us, running late. Ralph stopped to discuss the plan and they decided to drive to Rowter Farm and walk over to the entrance from there. The plan was to descend Titan and exit via Speedwell, for which Ralph had access permission and the key to the gate in the 'Far Canal' of Speedwell Mine.

Ralph drove uphill from Castleton and then along the rough track to Hurdlow. He parked near the gate to the fields in which the Titan entrance was situated. A cold wind blew across the tops and a cloudy sky did not bode well for the weather, so we all wanted to get underground as soon as possible. We quickly changed into our caving gear, walked across the field into the valley below and then climbed uphill to the entrance, now so well landscaped as to be almost invisible. My knees behaved well, without the usual aid of walking poles, thanks to the Diclofenac. The 46 metre deep entrance shaft that had taken four years to dig out was now lidded. Ralph undid the lid and Paul took a few photos of us preparing to descend. Then Sharon, as the youngest and most photogenic member, abseiled down inside the concrete piping that lined the shaft. Ralph, who wanted to take some shots for his video, went down next. I followed, but discovered that the thick, dry, rope had to be fed through my rack, slowing my descent and making it harder work than I had expected. 'Steve' descended next, followed by Paul, who was very glad to get out of the cold wind. Once Ralph had videoed us in the bedding plane that connected the entrance shaft to the top of the Titan shaft, Sharon clipped in to the topmost rope on Titan and began her descent to 'The Event Horizon', situated just over half way down.

It was my first visit, so I took great care at the top of the shaft. I clipped my long 'cow's-tail' into the traverse rope and sat down on the brink of the pitch. The vast dome and huge pit of Titan loomed in front of me, atmospheric, silent and eternally black, with a cold air of depth. This quite impressed me, but, in contrast, as I looked around me, I saw that the ledge, on which I was sitting, was beautifully decorated with stalagmites and yellowish flowstone. It was comfortable to sit on too, and provided with useful handholds that enabled me to reach the descent rope, attached to two bolts overhead by a 'Y-hang'. I apprehensively peered over the edge, having heard awful tales of cavers getting stuck on the bolt change at 'The Event Horizon' far below. I could glimpse Sharon's tiny spark of light as she abseiled soundlessly down to the end of the rope. The shaft was so large and sound-absorbing that I could barely hear her voice at 'The Event Horizon' as she shouted that the rope was free. I threaded my rack into the rope, checked it was safe, unclipped my long 'cow's-tail' from the traverse line and launched myself into space. I had descended many deep pitches before, but this was very exciting! The blackness of the vast shaft yawned below me and, as I cautiously descended, I felt as if I was in the middle of nowhere. I imagine that space explorers must have this sensation, too. The rope was thinner than the first one and ran smoothly through my rack, so I had a fairly rapid and easy descent through the dark emptiness of the huge shaft. As I slid down to the end of the rope, I saw that there was a short traverse line anchored to the wall. This rope led across to the edge of 'The Event Horizon' situated 62 metres above the bottom of the pitch.

Sharon was waiting at the end of the ledge, having descended the traverse rope as far as the anchors holding the lowermost Titan rope. I clipped my long 'cow's-tail' in to one of the bolts anchoring the traverse line, removed my rack from the upper rope and shouted that the rope was free. Securely clipped in, Sharon and I chatted quietly in the numinous of the surrounding vastness. It was quite cosy and companionable, but Ralph was ready to come down so we could not hang around for long! Sharon crossed the free-hanging bolt-change and descended the last pitch. I threaded my rack into the connecting rope and carefully worked my way down to the lip. Just as Sharon disappeared from view, Ralph arrived at the end of the rope on the ledge above me. Sharon shouted that she was at the bottom, so I began changing my rack over to the last rope. For a while, I was in a tiny world of my own, concentrating on the job in hand, lost in time and space. This side of The Planck Threshold, however, time exists, but it often seems to shrink and dilate depending on what one is doing. Minutes seemed to be compressed into micro-seconds as I assessed what to do. The change-over was not against the wall, but in mid-air. Tricky! There was a sling that could be used as a foot-loop dangling from a hanger, there was a piece of spare rope with a loop in it and a carabiner clipped into the '*Y-knot*' anchoring the bottom rope, too. I had several options to choose from! I hesitated, trying to decide whether to change my original plan or not, very aware of where I was. I was at the still point…

"Are you OK?" Ralph shouted, bringing me back into the real world.

"Yes! I'm taking my time, though!" I replied as I quickly decided what to do.

I clipped my short '*cow's-tail*' into the carabiner in the '*Y-knot*' and descended past it until the '*cow's-tail*' held my weight. I peered into the darkness to see the lower rope. It was navy blue and almost invisible! I clipped my hand-jammer, with its foot loop attached, into the lower rope, just below the knot, leaving enough space to be able to remove it later. Then I undid my rack from the top rope and threaded it into the navy blue rope, below the jammer. I pulled up some slack from below and used it to tie off my rack so that it would not move until I was ready to descend. Then I put a foot into the foot-loop and, with an arm around the rope to give me balance, heaved myself up to unclip my short '*cow's-tail*' from the belay. Lots of unfortunate cavers had become stuck or had major difficulties performing this particular manoeuvre! However, with my wire-gate carabiner and past practice, all went well and I was able to lower myself and transfer my weight on to my rack successfully. Satisfied that the rack was holding me, I kicked my foot out of the foot-loop and released the jammer, letting it hang by its security cord from my sit-harness. I had passed 'The Event Horizon'!

I untied the rack and, controlling its braking with my hand on the rope below it, let it slide down the rope. It was soon running smoothly as I let it accelerate down the navy blue rope. As I approached the bottom, there was a small bonus; some spray to cool the rack, lubricate the rope and get inside my neck. Once down, I disengaged my rack and shouted up to Ralph that the rope was free. Then I joined Sharon, sitting comfortably on a boulder well away from the pitch. We sat back to watch Ralph's descent, performed professionally with no problems. Ralph then videoed 'Steve' and Paul as they descended. He used very powerful floodlights that gave Sharon and me superb views up the enormous shaft. Once they were down and the video gear packed, our fun was over… Now it was time for the hard work!

'Steve' and Sharon led the way on down into a large boulder ruckle. The start was through a lozenge shaped, flat out, crawl with a smooth floor. "So far, so good!" I thought, as I wriggled through it. Lots more wriggling and thrutching between boulders followed, until we reached some scaffold poles supporting the boulders. This was a good sign as we then knew that we were on the right route. At one point further on, there was a vertical squeeze down through the bed-rock. I dislike this sort of squeeze because, if it contracts as you descend, you can get stuck! I hesitated and shouted to 'Steve' below for re-assurance. "Just relax and you'll slide through OK!" He shouted to me. As another 'older caver', I trusted 'Steve's' advice and did as he said. I lowered my feet into the squeeze and, taking my weight on my arms, lowered my legs into the crack and slid downwards. My hips stuck immediately! I wriggled them free and slowly sank deeper into the squeeze until my chest stuck quite firmly! "Uh-Oh!" I thought. I paused, exhaled, kicked my legs and, scraping my chest, wriggled free to drop into the passage below. "I hope that's the last of that sort of thing!" I breathed as 'Steve' stopped me from falling. I had not been warned about this bit, probably on purpose to make sure that I did not chicken out of the trip!

After that excitement, it was good to have a short spell of upright movement until we came to the small stream in the 'Far Peak Extension'. Here, we branched right into a low, very muddy crawl with a deep pool in it that we had to pass on our stomachs. Not pleasant but relatively easy! The crawl ended in a passage, followed by a few vertical climbs up fixed steel ladders. Everything here was very muddy and rather gloomy as there were no reflections from the walls to light our way. We were soon well coated with mud, too. 'Steve' was leading and pointed out the stemples high above in 'Stemple Highway'; another route marker. There were more muddy crawls and some traversing above a rift, luckily with muddy hand-lines to clip into for protection. A final low, gritty, crawl, with two U-bends in it, each a third full of muddy water, was a most unpleasant finale. We emerged from this into the large chamber at the base of the 'Leviathan'. This is the last pitch in the James Hall Over Engine Mine (JH) that was first descended after seven years of research and digging by Dave Nixon. 'JH' subsequently gave access to the route that led to the discovery of the Titan shaft on the first of January 1999. Here, there were things to sit on, so we paused for a breather before climbing down through the scaffolded 'Boulder Pile' to the Speedwell Stream-way. What a pleasure it was to clean off the mud, de-grit ourselves and see clearly!

We sat on the rocks for a while, eating our snacks and chatting, before setting off along the stream-way. The water level was mostly below the tops of our wellies except in one or two refreshingly deep places. Soon we were at the 'Whirlpool', a serious obstacle in flood conditions as it really is a whirlpool then. We passed over this balanced on the cables fixed to the wall near water level. These had been placed in situ to avoid a wetting, but, at the far end, there was no avoiding an immersion to above the waist in icy water. Wading steadily, we were soon past 'Pit-prop Passage' and at 'The Bung' passage, to the left. 'The Bung' is the wet pitch that has to be descended to exit via Peak Cavern. It looked very wet! I was glad that we were not taking that route, needless to say! We soon reached the locked gate in the 'Far Canal' that gives access to the show cave. Ralph had a key and quickly opened it for us to continue to the end of the 'Far Canal'. We climbed out of this, slightly out of breath and dripping wet, into the chamber above 'The Bottomless Pit' of Speedwell Mine. Here, there was a large group of tourists, waiting for a boat to take them back out to the Speedwell show cave entrance. Their guide made capital out of our sudden arrival and very kindly made space for three of us in the boat. It was 'Age and Beauty first'! 'Steve' and Paul hung on behind the boat as it slowly ploughed its way along the final canal. At one point, 'Steve' and Paul had to wade as the propeller came out of the water! The draught in the tunnel was very cold, so we were all glad when the boat landed at the base of the Speedwell steps and discharged its passengers. With our wellies full of water and all of our clothes and gear sodden with water, the 105 steps up to daylight were hard work! Then it was a mile on foot to Castleton, or uphill to Rowter! The walk warmed us up in spite of the icy wind, but we were glad to arrive back at the TSG Chapel. The entrance changing room was heaving with smelly cavers, who had been on different trips from us, busily changing from their caving gear into their clean outdoor clothes. We quickly removed our muddy, wet, gear and changed into our everyday clothes. What a pleasure it was to be in dry clothes again! Along with the rest of 'The Crewe', we all went for pints of celebratory beer at 'The Castle' pub. The beer never tasted so good! We felt particularly pleased with ourselves, too. What a convivial end to an exciting and enjoyable traverse!

30
The Terminal Sump

Many limestone caves, especially those with active stream-ways, end in a terminal sump where the water continues on its way underground without an air-space. Unless the sump is short and reasonably roomy, this is often the limit of exploration for normal cavers, who can only free dive such obstacles. Even properly equipped cave divers may be unable to progress any further if the sump is too tight, or filled with silt, or loose rocks. Usually the water flowing through the sump may be traced, by dye, or biological markers, to its resurgence. If the distance to the resurgence is significant, attempts to pass the sump, or to enlarge it, may be made, but rarely with success. In most of these situations, the terminal sump will mark the end of the cave.

Older cavers will usually accept that the terminal sump is the end of the cave. It represents the limits of caving in that cave and even of caving life itself. As older cavers approach the terminal sump, they tend to be more risk-aware and to enjoy the preceding passages to the full, knowing that the terminal sump is always ahead of them. The terminal sump of life engulfs everyone eventually. Whereas the other side of a terminal sump in a cave can be deduced from tracing the flow of the water, the other side of the terminal sump of life remains a mystery. Occasional 'near-death' experiences have suggested that there is a light on the other side, but otherwise, there is no scientific means of discovering what is really there. It is the final unknown and the only certainty in life is that we shall all have our chance to explore it eventually.

The terminal sump of life has intrigued humanity since time immemorial and has resulted in the multitude of hypothetical explanations constructed by the different religions in the world. The terminal sump of life, however, is still a mystery. Buddhists believe that the terminal sump of life is only a change process to another life that will be repeated time and time again until 'Nirvana' is finally attained. The Judeo-Christian-Moslem faiths promise a paradise, or a hell, on the other side depending on the spiritual and moral performance of a person in their active life. Other religions have faith in their own predictions, but no ordinary human has ever returned to say what is on the other side. Whatever one's belief, it seems a good idea to try and find paradise here on earth. Perhaps that is what cavers are seeking subconsciously when they go exploring caves and potholes.

Death can occur at any age. It is not just the terminal sump for old cavers. However, the chance of dying obeys the Normal or Gaussian Probability Distribution that is used by statisticians. The curve of the Normal Distribution, with the number of people alive at a certain age plotted on the vertical axis and their age plotted on the horizontal axis, looks rather like a camel's hump. There is mean population value at the top of the hump that tapers down in a curve to meet the horizontal axis on either side. The Normal Distribution can be used to determine the probability of a person surviving to a particular age and is often used by life insurers to calculate premiums. There are most people alive at the hump in the middle and fewest at the tapered ends of the curve. For anyone interested in this subject there is a website run by The Office of National Statistics for the UK population on www.ons.gov.uk. In 2011, men in the UK lived to an average age of 85 and women to an average age of 89. Over the ten preceding years, the average age of survival increased by about ten years for men and eight for women. About 10% of the population were over the age of seventy, so there would appear to be plenty of time for older cavers to continue enjoying their chosen sport!

The main causes of death arise from two basic sources: naturally occurring hazards or man-made hazards. Natural hazards include illness, falling, drowning, suffocation and burning accidents as well as natural disasters such as tsunamis, earthquakes, hurricanes and lightning strikes. Man-made hazards include war, terrorism, murder, industrial or transport accidents, suicide and euthanasia. In Britain, the statistics indicate that most people die from diseases of one sort or another, with only about four per cent dying from other causes. The consequences of deaths resulting from all of these causes can differ widely, but can be categorised into four basic types. Death can be quick, or slow and at the same time it can be painless, or painful. Most people would choose a quick and painless death if they had the choice. Unfortunately most of us have no choice in this matter and have to endure whatever chance brings us!

There are, of course, fates worse than death. The tenacity, courage and sheer determination of the individuals who fight for their life in the most desperate circumstances and against all odds is one of the most incredible and admirable characteristics of the human race. However, not all people can fight a fate worse than death without a measure of despair. This raises the issues of suicide and euthanasia as potential ways of avoiding such fates. There are many examples of people committing suicide, or undergoing euthanasia, as a means of release from unbearable mental or physical agony. Conversely, there are many attempts to alleviate such suffering by the works of carers, the hospice movement, religious organisations and other bodies. The benefits and costs arising from these issues are outside the confines of this book, but there is no doubt that they are extremely important issues that will have to be faced by everyone at some time in their lives. This is when personal beliefs and attitudes are crucial to survival in peace. The inevitable passage to the terminal sump is rarely easy and requires considerable courage and stamina!

The death of an old friend, or close relative, always generates intense emotions and deep thoughts. Each of us is unique and the loss of one of us is a loss to everyone. A death re-unites all of those who knew the deceased. The funeral rites celebrate the life that has ended in a way that satisfies the human need to try and make sense of reality since time immemorial. The funeral also unites and re-unites, all of those who knew the deceased.

The human being is one of the most complex systems in our world and, like all complex systems, exhibits emergent properties that are often unexpected and surprisingly powerful. (The human society is an even more complex system with outcomes that range from charitable institutions and laws, to war and terrorism!) In other words: "The whole is greater than the sum of its parts". An individual will exhibit all sorts of personal characteristics as well as physical, mental and spiritual abilities, often without being fully aware of them. The personality radiates an aura that is perceived by friends and relations, depending on their own abilities and awareness. When a person dies, friends and relatives are likely to express and share their perceptions explicitly. It is in this way that people live on in the minds of the living. Whatever you believe, the dead will always have some impact on your life, long after their passing.

Nowadays, the spiritual life is often suppressed and smothered by the intense noise, materialism and haste of modern life. There are many people who do not consider the spiritual life to be of any value, but it is amazing how such people radiate their own spirituality so strongly when decrying it! The intense sorrow at a death, the awe and wonder precipitated by 'the green flash' of a tropical sunset, the view from a high mountain, the icy beauty of a snow scene, the ecstasy of music, mescalin and madness, the sight of an unexplored cavern, all prompt an awareness of our own spiritual nature. Cavers often experience this awareness in their adventures underground. It is probably the reason that they find the caving lifestyle so rewarding and inspiring.

Alongside the issues just raised, there is the issue of risking one's life for personal gain, or pleasure. Although soldiering, exploration, experiment and dangerous sports have been practised since human life began, there is still a large body of opinion that would like to ban, or control them. Again, it is a very personal decision to embark on a potentially fatal adventure and the reasons may not always be clear to external observers. Explorers, horse-riders, motorcyclists, car racers, rock climbers, skiers, parachute jumpers and cavers, obtain such inspiration and buzz from their risk-taking that, to them, the outcome makes it worth the effort.

Caving accident statistics suggest that caving is about as risky as motorcycling and is less risky than rock-climbing, or mountaineering. Cavers do not take needless risks anyway. Great care and attention is given to the preparation of equipment and to rigging vertical obstacles. Cavers always carry reserve lighting with them as there is no way of overcoming the absolute and eternal darkness of caves without a light. The clothes and specialised garments used by cavers also give protection from hypothermia. Caver's local knowledge of their cave systems is of great benefit, especially in stream-ways that can flood. Dry escape routes, or havens, have saved many cavers from a watery death in the past. The calculated risks that cavers take are especially applicable to older cavers. By the time that a caver is considered to be an 'older caver', experience will enable risks to be well controlled, even if there are then additional risks of health problems due to age. Caving is a sport that inspires cavers without the attentions of 'The Health & Safety Brigade' and long may it continue to be so!

Perhaps Edward Fitzgerald's paraphrase of the Rubáiyát of the twelfth century Persian poet, Omar Khayyám, gives food for thought at this point:

"*The Moving Finger writes; and, having writ,*
Moves on: nor all thy Piety nor Wit
Shall lure it back to cancel half a Line,
Nor all thy Tears wash out a Word of it."
So, just keep going! Bon Voyage!

Appendix 1

Probability of getting at least one six in two throws of a dice = 11/36
(*See Truth Table below*)
Probability of being struck by lightning in the UK = approx. 1 in ten million per person per year.
Probability of being killed by a meteorite = 1 in 100 Billion per person per year.
Probability of winning a Premium Bond prize = approx. 1 in 26,000 per bond per month.
Probability of winning UK National Lottery = approx. 1 in 14 Million per ticket per week.

Truth Table for two throws of a dice:
First Throw: Second Throw: Probability of this result: At least one six?

First Throw	Second Throw	Probability of this result:	At least one six?
6	1 to 5	$1/6 \times 5/6 = 5/36$	Yes
6	6	$1/6 \times 1/6 = 1/36$	Yes
1 to 5	6	$5/6 \times 1/6 = 5/36$	Yes
1 to 5	1 to 5	$5/6 \times 5/6 = 25/36$	No

Total = 36/36 = 1 Checks all possibilities certain
The probability that at least one six is thrown in the two throws = 5/36+1/36+5/36= 11/36

Glossary of Terms

Ascender: A device for ascending a single rope, usually working on the principle of a cam that jams in the rope so that, whilst the ascender can be pushed up the rope freely, it cannot be pulled down. Using two ascenders, one for the chest and one for the feet, it is possible to ascend a rope by moving the ascenders one at a time. (*Also see 'Hand-jammer'*)

Aven: An overhead shaft above a cave passage, usually connecting with an upper series.

Bedding Plane: An enlarged lateral joint between two beds of limestone, or in a shale band. Usually a bedding plane is wide and low.

Belay: A rock pillar, stalagmite boss, large boulder, or a hole in the rock, to which a ladder or rope can be attached securely. Artificial belays, or anchors, are made by drilling a hole into a rock-face and inserting a metal ring, or other attachment, for the same purpose.

Breccia: A geological term for broken rock and angular stones cemented together by calcite or lime.

Calcite: A crystalline deposit of Calcium Carbonate.

Carabiner: A metal snap-link for connecting to ropes, or to a belay. Also used for connecting climbing devices to the caver's equipment.

Cave Rescue: Cave rescue is provided underground by teams from local caving clubs. The surface call-outs and ambulance arrangements are organised by the local police force.

Cow's-tail: A length of rope or tape used to protect the caver when performing manoeuvres such as passing a belay, or traversing a hand-line. The caver usually has two cows-tails, a short one for attaching to a belay when descending a rope and a long one for passing a belay when ascending.

Deflection Belay: A belay that is used to pull the rope away from a potential rubbing point. The main rope runs through a carabiner clipped into a tape, or short rope loop, attached to an anchor in a wall away from a rub point.

Descender: A device for descending a single rope. The device acts as a brake to control the descent and can become hot on a long descent. There are several types of descender in use by cavers. The rack, using alloy bars, is often used for very long descents. (*See Rack*)

Duck: A cave passage almost filled with water, but with just enough air-space to allow breathing.

Existentialist: A person who holds an anti-intellectualist philosophy of life, holding that man is free and responsible, based on the assumption that reality as existence can only be lived but can never be the object of thought.

Flowstone: A continuous sheet of calcite on a wall, floor, or rocks, formed by the deposition from slowly flowing water rich in calcium carbonate.

Gour: A formation around the rim of a pool, or basin, deposited from water rich in calcium carbonate over-flowing the rim. The pool deepens as the gour, or rimstone, builds up to form a 'Gour Pool'.

Hand-jammer: A slang term for a hand-held ascender. (*See Poignée*)

Helictite: An eccentric stalactite, or stalagmite, that has elements growing out at various angles to the axis, or with branches that are usually curved and twisted.

Moon-milk: A soft and friable form of calcite sometimes found on the floor of cave passages.

Nirvana: The ultimate objective of Buddhists, that is, to become one with the universe. Enlightenment.

Pitch: A vertical section of cave, or a drop normally passed by using a ladder, or a rope, if it is too difficult to climb down. Sometimes referred to as a shaft.

Poignée: A handled ascender used for climbing up a single rope.

Rack: A type of descender that has several alloy braking bars through which the rope is threaded to provide controlled braking during a descent.

Re-belay: An artificial belay placed at some point along a rope to avoid abrasion, or water. A re-belay has to be passed when descending by removing the descender from the section of rope above the re-belay and re-inserting the descender into the section of the rope after the re-belay. During this manoeuvre, the caver attaches himself, or herself, to the re-belay by a short piece of rope, or tape, termed a ' Cow's-tail'. The reverse procedure is followed for the ascent.

Resurgence: The point at which an underground stream emerges at the surface.

Selenite: A crystalline form of Gypsum (Hydrated Calcium Sulphate)

Sink: The point at which a surface stream sinks below the surface.

Straw: A hollow, thin-walled stalactite that has the same diameter along its length and looks like a straw. Straws are very fragile.

Stream-way: A cave passage occupied by flowing water.

Sump: A cave passage completely filled with water. Long sumps are passed using diving equipment.

Siphon: The French word for a sump.

Tao: The inexpressible source of being. The principle that underlies and controls the world. A cardinal principle of Taoist thought is that it is through inaction that true results are obtained.

Tourist: A visitor on a guided tour. (*A word sometimes used resentfully by xenophobes.*)

Traverse: A horizontal section, or movement, along a cave passage at some distance above the floor, or along a wall

Wet-suit: A skin-tight suit of foamed neoprene rubber that provides thermal insulation, but allows water in. Although the wearer becomes wet when immersed in water, the wet-suit effect keeps the wearer warm.

Y-Hang: A rope belay in the shape of a 'Y', attached to two artificial rock anchors so that the load on the rope is evenly distributed between the two anchors.

Y-Knot: A knot tied in a rope so that it can be used for a 'Y-Hang' between two artificial anchors in the rock-face.

Lightning Source UK Ltd.
Milton Keynes UK
UKOW05f0628260913

217951UK00001B/9/P